Withdrawn

BEST BEACH

GAMES

BARRY COLEMAN

Pineapple Press, Inc.
Sarasota, Florida

W9-DGV-940

Pineapple Press, Inc.
P.O. Box 3889
Sarasota, Florida 34230

www.pineapplepress.com

Library of Congress Cataloging-in-Publication Data

Coleman, Barry,
    Best beach games / Barry Coleman.
        p. cm.
    ISBN 978-1-56164-590-9 (pbk. : alk. paper)
  1. Outdoor recreation. 2. Outdoor games. 3. Beaches. I. Title.
    GV191.62.C65 2013
    796.5'3--dc23
                                                    2012040622

First Edition
10 9 8 7 6 5 4 3 2 1

Printed in the United States

TABLE OF CONTENTS

Introduction   8

Beach Lingo   10

What You Need   12

Before You Go   14

Tips to Keep Everyone Safe   16

Beach Etiquette   18

Choosing Teams   20

Who Goes First?   22

      Rock-Paper-Scissors   22

      Upstairs or Downstairs   24

I. Time ☞ 26

    1. Family Sand Silhouettes   28

    2. Beach Obstacle Course   30

    3. Two-Minute Drill   32

    4. Which Way Is North?   34

    5. Tell Time without a Clock   36

    6. Fill the Bucket   38

    7. Beach Blanket Bingo   40

    8. Beach Blanket Magic   42

    9. Pass the Shell   44

II. Water ☞ 46

    10. Drip-Drip-Dump 48

    11. Ping-Pong Ball Race 50

    12. Private Tidal Pool 52

13. Drizzle Castle 54

14. Saltwater Race 56

15. Will It Float? 58

16. Tip of the Iceberg 60

17. Where Did Our Stuff Go? 62

III. Earth   64

18. The Sand beneath Your Feet 66

19. Saturate the Sand 68

20. Sand Town 70

21. Sort the Shells 72

22. Walk on the Wild Side 74

23. Scavenger Hunt 76

24. Beach Alphabet 78

25. Indian Kickball 80

IV. Wind   82

26. Ring Toss 84

27. Sand Darts 86

28. Edisto Roll 88

29. Bouncy Tennis Basketball 90

30. Four Corners of Roll 92

31. First to Fifty 94

32. Ribbon Dancing 96

V. Low Tide   98

33. Folly Field Roll 100

34. Baseball Shuffleboard 102

35. Coastal Bowling 104

36. Dots to Boxes 106

37. Capture the Shark 108

38. Sand Badminton   110

39. Whales and Minnows   112

40. Tic-Tac-Toe   114

41. Expanded Tic-Tac-Toe   116

42. Three in a Row   118

VI. High Tide   120

43. Dizzy Race   122

44. Run for the Flounder   124

45. Musical Sit-Down   126

46. Nim   128

47. Pick Up the Sticks   130

48. Pickle (a.k.a. Rundown)   132

49. String Hunt for Treasure   134

50. X Marks the Spot   136

51. Treasure Hunt   138

VII. Dice and Marble Games   140

52. Seashell Around the Clock   142

53. Free the Dolphin   144

54. 100-Yard Dash   146

55. Speedway   148

56. Dare to Risk It   150

57. Poker Dice   152

58. Going to the Jersey Shore   154

59. Shoot the Marbles   156

60. Marble through the Mountain   158

61. Marble to the Edge 160

62. Marble Bocce   162

VIII. If You Brought It . . . ✐ 164

    63. Golf 166

    64. Putt-Putt 168

    65. Roll Back 170

    66. Bicycle Coast Race 172

    67. Tennis at the Beach 174

    68. Sand Sock Volleyball 176

    69. Flip the Cup 178

    70. Crabbing 180

IX. Try This at Home ✐ 182

    71. Design a Dry Garden 184

    72. Ocean in a Bottle 186

    73. Float an Egg 188

    74. Let's See Density in Action 190

    75. Ocean Currents 192

    76. Make Your Own Sea Salt 194

    77. The Water Cycle 196

Recommended Reading 198

ACKNOWLEDGMENTS

As a novice writer who started out with nothing but an idea for a book, I would like to thank Elaine Adcox, Kim Flory, Kim Bayne Townsend, and Donna Smith for their editorial help. I would also like to thank my friends from the Greenville Emrys Foundation, who showed me how to narrow the focus of this book. I also owe a huge thank you to Pam Zollman for her guidance and wisdom and for introducing me to the best editor I could have had, Rebecca Davis. Rebecca, you are a novice writer's dream. Thanks so much. Rich Nicoloff, thanks for teaching me more about a camera in two hours than I had learned in a lifetime.

I also owe a big thank you to Charlie, Dawn, and Mark Stewart from Folly Beach, along with Wallace Kelley on Edisto Island, who shared not only their homes but their advice on coastal living. Thanks also to the families who joined in the fun with my family on many different beaches for your insight on how to improve the games.

June Cussen, thank you so much for giving this book a chance. Thanks also to your professional staff, including Shé Hicks and Kris Rowland, who is an extraordinary editor.

I would like to thank my parents, Bill and Margaret Coleman, for introducing me to the Atlantic Coast.

The biggest thanks of all go to my beautiful wife and best friend for 36 years, Tamala Coleman. Tam, your patience, guidance, and understanding allowed this book to happen. To my sons, Doug and Wil—it has been a blast hanging out with you boys. I love each of you with all my heart.

INTRODUCTION

Children love playing games, especially when it means spending more time with their parents. Games also give us a reason to unplug our electronics in a beautiful outdoor setting. Now more than ever it's important to get children outside to see, smell, touch, and breathe in nature's wonder. Aside from an increased attention span, children receive many benefits from playing games, including learning how to take turns, be considerate of others, follow rules, and win and lose graciously.

On family vacations with our two small sons, my wife would turn me into a pack mule, hauling loads of stuff to and from the beach. Knowing there was a better way to entertain our kids, I thought back to my early years on a small farm in Travelers Rest, South Carolina, and adapted the games from my childhood to the coastal environment. Now we use mostly what's on hand at the beach when we get there, along with some lightweight odds and ends that we haul in a single beach bucket.

When people first looked at our family playing with marbles, tennis balls, and socks filled with sand, we could almost see them thinking, *These people need some serious therapy.* But after watching for a bit, they would approach us and ask if they could join in. And something else remarkable happened as well: People actually started talking to each other.

Some of the activities in this book are competitive, while others emphasize cooperation, but there is nothing passive about any of them. The majority of them are aimed at children aged 2 to 10, with a few thrown in for teenagers. The best thing is that most of the games and activities require nothing more than items found naturally on the beach. So take advantage of the tips I've picked up on vacations at more than 70 different beaches. Have fun with the kids, and remember—the sand will wash off, but the memories will last forever.

BEACH LINGO

Beach debris – any natural debris washed onto the beach such as coral, driftwood, salt hay, and shells

Comb the beach – Search the beach for items to use in games and activities.

Driftwood – lengths of wood found on the beach. If none are available, you can substitute salt hay or a wooden dowel.

Falling tide – the transition period between high tide and low tide

Grid – a series of squares linked together. The grid can vary from 4 to 40 squares in a rectangular or square shape.

High tide – When the ocean is at its highest level, the area available for play is smaller.

Low tide – When the ocean is at its lowest point, it creates the day's widest beach. The sand is softest near the water and becomes much harder as you move away from the water (until you reach the soft sand area).

Marker – a shell used to mark your spot in games. You can customize your shell with a permanent marker.

Salt hay – any type of grass, such as dune grass, cordgrass, or sea oats, that has washed up onto the beach. Use the stalks to mark holes in the sand. Do not pick any living beach grasses.

Sand sock – Fill a sock two-fifths of the way full with dry sand. Pinch the sock with your fingers just above the sand, spin it around a couple of times, and pull the remainder of the sock back over itself. Polyester socks stay dryer than cotton socks.

Soft sand – the deep, dry, soft sand found above the tidal zone or wrack line

Tally mark – a way to keep score. Draw a straight line in the sand for each win up to four. With the fifth win, draw a diagonal line across the four straight lines.

Tidal sand – the smooth, packed sand that is covered during high tide and exposed during low tide

Treasure – any sort of bright and shiny manmade things such as balls, coins, marbles, and plastic toys. Please be sure to take treasure home with you when you leave the beach.

Wrack line – the line of debris washed up by previous tides. There are often three wrack lines: the last high tide, the last spring tide, and the last storm surge.

WHAT YOU NEED

For most of the games in this book, you can simply use items normally found on any beach. Others require that you bring a few items from home. I suggest you decide which games interest you the most and then plan accordingly. Remember, everything you'll need for a week of play needs to fit in a beach bucket.

- Baseball – Any baseball works fine, but the cheaper ones with a synthetic cover tend to stay dryer.
- Dice – Children may enjoy the bigger ones designed to hang from a car's rearview mirror.

- Food coloring – A mixture of shaving cream and vinegar will remove it from your hands.
- Frisbee
- Marbles – Make sure you have a large "shooter" marble along with the smaller ones.
- Permanent marker
- Ping-Pong balls
- Plastic bucket
- Ribbon (optional) – Use to wrap around beach debris to mark holes in the sand.
- Sand sock
- Tennis balls
- Tide chart – You can find charts in the free coastal magazine racks outside beachside storefronts.
- Treasure
- White vinegar
- Wooden dowels (3/8-inch diameter)

BEFORE YOU GO

There's nothing worse than settling into your beach chair only to realize you've forgotten something.

- Thirty minutes before you leave your house or hotel, apply a high-SPF, waterproof sunscreen on each person. Don't forget ears, hands, necks, and tops of the feet. Pack or rent an umbrella to keep children less than a year old completely out of the sun.

- If a beach badge is required for your beach, be sure to take it with you.

- Be sure everyone has a hat, flip-flops or shoes, a shirt, and good sunglasses. If your kids are younger, try thick, fuzzy winter socks, which will keep their feet safe from the hot sand and are easier to walk in than flip-flops.

- Take a cooler with enough water and juice to keep everyone hydrated for the day. Try freezing a few non-carbonated drinks and grapes, which will chill the other items in the cooler. You'll use less ice and can carry a smaller cooler.

- Take bed sheets to sit on. They dry more quickly than towels.

- Glance at your tide chart and make a mental note of the times of high and low tide.

- Take money for the umbrella rental and the ice cream vendor.

- Take a small, zipper-lock plastic bag to keep cell phones, camera, money, and keys dry and sand free.

- Carry sand toys in a mesh bag, which is also handy for carrying trash and shells home.

- If you drive to the beach, pack a gallon of water or a container of baby powder with cornstarch to keep sand out of the car. Either rinse everyone's feet with water or shake the powder onto damp feet. After a moment the sand easily brushes away.

TIPS TO KEEP EVERYONE SAFE

- The locals' best-kept secret is to not arrive at the beach until later in the day. Even if you arrive at 4:00 p.m., you'll still have about 5 hours of sunlight left. Not only do you miss the crowds but also the most damaging ultraviolet rays. Keep in mind, however, that lifeguards often leave the beach at 5:00 p.m.

- Make sure everyone knows the name and beach marker number of the hotel or inn where you're staying.

- Have everyone wear flip-flops, fuzzy socks, or sandals on the way to the beach.

- Reapply sunscreen and lip balm on everyone every hour or so and always after swimming.

- Be sure everyone stays hydrated by drinking juice or water every thirty minutes or so.

- On a very crowded beach, personalize your area by making a family flag from a pillowcase.

- Check with the lifeguard to see if there are any dangerous conditions present. Always swim with a buddy, and when weather conditions are in doubt, don't go out. Remember, an absence of signs or a flag doesn't mean it's safe to swim. If you have smaller children, stay near the lifeguard, but don't expect him or her to supervise your children.

- Teach everyone the "stingray shuffle": As you walk through the water, shuffle your feet through the sand, creating vibrations to spook the shy stingrays and skates into swimming away before you step on them.

- Never swim near groins, jetties, and piers or dive in shallow water.

- Don't turn your back to the waves, which can quickly rise up and knock you down.

- Remind everyone how to "break the grip of the rip": Stay calm, raise your arm, and yell to other swimmers that you're caught in a rip current. If you're a strong swimmer, you can escape the current by swimming parallel to the shoreline.

- Warn children not to touch anything that looks like a plastic bag; it could be a jellyfish.

- Be watchful of toddlers anytime they are around water.

- When children run away, they tend to follow the path of least resistance, so follow the wind when searching for them.

- After a day at the beach, clean children's fingernails and wash their hands with antibacterial soap.

BEACH
ETIQUETTE

- Carry your supplies for the day in mesh or canvas bags instead of plastic (except for a small plastic bag to protect cell phones, camera, money, and keys). A plastic bag can end up in the ocean where a sea turtle may mistake it for one of his favorite foods, a jellyfish.

- Carefully check the local beach rules, usually posted on the beach access path. Some beaches, such as those in South Walton, Florida, prohibit the removal of both sand and water.

- Keep a respectable distance from your neighbors.

- When you generate trash, automatically place it in your cooler or mesh bag. Recycle everything you can, and dispose of the rest in a trash can that is not already overflowing.

- Never take glass containers to the beach.

- If you smoke, please be considerate about secondhand smoke. Dispose of cigarette butts in your own trash, not in the sand.

- Offer to watch your neighbors' stuff if they go for a swim; they'll do the same for you.

- Don't feed the cute little bird. It will only draw hundreds of his friends, and your beach neighbors will not be happy with you.

- If you dig holes in the sand, keep them shallow, mark them with beach debris, and fill them in before you leave. You wouldn't want a baby sea turtle to get stuck in the hole as he attempts to crawl toward his new life in the ocean.

- If you didn't build the sand castle, you can't knock it down.
- If you bring a radio, keep the volume turned down. The big guy in the cowboy hat may not like heavy metal music.
- Never shake the sand from your beach towel near other people.
- Stay on marked paths, and never go into the dunes to play. On many beaches it is illegal to pick, harm, or destroy sea oats.
- Don't harm or take home any animal life including birds, conchs, crabs, and sand dollars.
- The best advice remains "Take only pictures; leave only footprints."

CHOOSING TEAMS

There is no joy in being on a losing team every time. You could have the captains pick the teams, but someone invariably gets his feelings hurt every time. There are the natural teams, such as adults versus kids and boys versus girls, but there are times when it makes more sense to have evenly matched teams.

- If you have a really diverse group, one method is to have everyone line up from the shortest to the tallest and have each person count off "one" or "two" down the line. The ones will be on one team, the twos on the other. While not perfect, this method does ensure there is an even number of short and tall people on both teams.

- For an even number of players, such as eight teenagers, place four white shells and four dark shells in a hat and let each player blindly pick a shell. The white shells are on one team, the dark shells on the other.

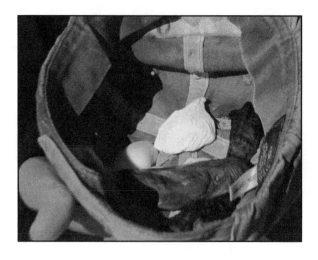

- Another method to pick two teams is to play Rock-Paper-Scissors (see next page for instructions), but leave off the Paper. The players who throw Rock are on one team, Scissors on the other. It may take a few times to get even numbers for each team, but it's possible. To get three evenly matched teams, add the Paper back in.

Did you know the "Sanibel Stoop" is the nickname given to visitors to Sanibel Island, Florida, who are constantly doubled over while picking up shells?

WHO GOES FIRST?

Rock-Paper-Scissors

Use this game to save time and tears to determine who goes first in a game. Contrary to what many people think, when experienced R-P-S players take each other on, it's not a game of chance or luck. It's actually a game of intelligence, observation, and strategy.

Ages: 6 and up
Number of participants: 2–3

- The players stand facing each other or in a circle where everyone can see each other's hands. Each player balls one hand into a fist and pounds it into the other hand, chanting, "One, two, three." On three, the players show their chosen symbol.

- The options are to leave your hand in a fist like a rock, lay it flat like paper, or stick the middle and index fingers out like scissors. Now it's time to sort the results.

  - Rock beats scissors by dulling them.
  - Scissors beats paper by cutting it.
  - Paper beats rock by covering it.

- For three players, follow these rules. If two players throw rock and one player throws scissors, scissors is out and the two rocks play each other to decide a winner. If one player throws paper and two throw rock, paper wins. If two players throw paper and one throws scissors, scissors is the winner. If each player throws a different symbol, play again.

Did you know Egypt's great pyramids contain thousands of seashells in their structure? This is because the pyramids were built with limestone, which formed during the Cretaceous period (145 to 65 million years ago) when Egypt was underneath the sea.

23

Upstairs or Downstairs

This is a quick way to determine who goes first in a 2-player game.

Ages: 6 and up

Number of participants: 2

You'll need:
- 1 small shell

How to Play:
- One player places his hands behind his back and hides the shell in either his left or right hand.
- He brings his hands to the front of his body and moves

them around hocus-pocus style before placing one hand on top of the other. He then asks, "Where is the shell, upstairs or downstairs?"

- The second player guesses which hand holds the shell.
- The player holding the shell opens the guessed hand. If the shell falls out, the guesser goes first. If not, the player holding the shell goes first. To be sure the shell holder is not playing a "shell game," he must show the shell in the other hand.

You can also play this as a stand-alone game. Just play to a predetermined number of correct guesses to decide the winner.

Did you know the largest active sand dune on the Eastern Seaboard is the Jockey's Ridge sand dune located on the Outer Banks of North Carolina? It is estimated the Jockey's Ridge dune contains 6 million dump-truck loads of mostly quartz sand granules. ✍

I.
TIME

The real world is in the rearview mirror. It's time for a coastal state of mind as you head with your family to where the sand meets the water. It's time to put away your worries and visit your favorite summertime destination. It's time to relax, kick back, sleep late, and come together with your family in a way not possible at home.

Look at this vacation as a chance to unplug the electronics and spend time outside with the kids, play games, do silly activities, and actually talk to each other. The following activities and games all involve time in one way or another. Use them to make the most of the short time you have together, because all too soon it will be time to head home.

Did you know at the peak of the Last Great Ice Age, only 21,000 years ago, sea level was 330 feet lower? This means the spot where you're standing on the beach right now would have been, depending on the slope of the continental shelf, 30 to 70 miles inland from the ocean.

1

Family Sand Silhouettes

Use this activity to see what your family and friends really think about the way you look.

Ages: 2 and up

Number of participants: any

You'll need:
- beach debris
- camera

How to Play:
- Comb the beach for objects to be used to represent facial and body features, such as large whelk shells, seaweed, tiny shells, sea grass, etc.

- In the damp intertidal sand, have one person lie on his back with his arms and legs extended. With a shell, trace a deep outline of his body in the sand, including head, arms, and legs.

- Use your imagination to complete the silhouette. Use seaweed for hair, clamshells for eyeglasses, pink shells for fingernails, and small white shells for teeth. Exaggerate personal features, such as a whelk shell for a large nose, salt hay for long fingers, and tiny shells for small ears.

- After the first silhouette is done, have another person lie next to it and repeat the process. When everyone's silhouette is finished, take a picture of this timeless and unique family portrait to hang in your home.

As long as you used natural items, leave the portraits for others to admire. The ocean will erase the silhouettes with the next high tide.

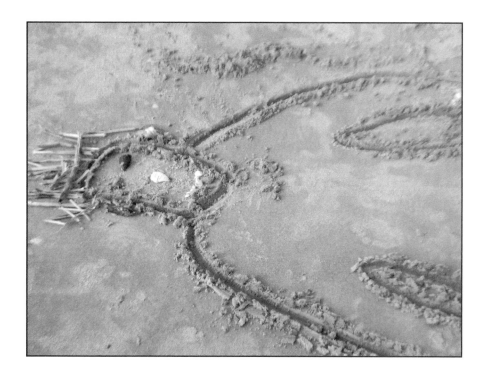

Did you know when sand squeaks as you walk on it, the sound you hear is tiny shells and pebbles rubbing against each other?

2
Beach Obstacle Course

Helping young children construct an obstacle course can build their self-esteem.

Ages: 2–4

Number of participants: 1 or more

You'll need:
- beach debris

How to Play:
- With a shell, draw a winding, 50-foot-long road in the damp tidal sand by drawing two parallel lines about 2 feet apart. Route a portion of the road into the wave swash, even though the lines will disappear. Children will enjoy splashing in the water, then looking for the link back to the road.

- Work with your children to place obstacles such as driftwood and shells to hop over. In one section, narrow the road width to 3 inches and line it with shells, forcing children to walk through heel-to-toe. Also scoop out a few 1-inch-deep gullies to jump over. Consider the children's abilities to decide how wide to make these gullies. If you're lucky enough to have a shallow tidal pool nearby, try to incorporate it into the road as well.

- If the children are small and the sand compacts well, build a small mound for them to jump or walk over. Build the

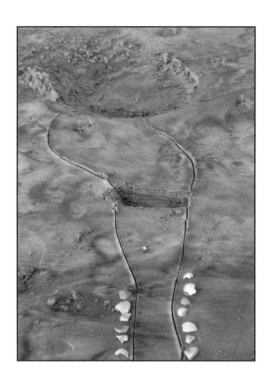

mound no bigger than 6 inches tall and 1 foot wide. If possible, build a slope on one side to walk up and let them jump off the other side.

- At the end of the road, draw a simple hopscotch grid to hop through.

- You can discreetly time the children to see if they get faster each time around the course.

Did you know the world's only sea without a shoreline lies off the coast of the southeastern United States? The Sargasso Sea isn't defined by land but by ocean currents. Great Lake eels come here to spawn, and many baby loggerhead turtles spend their early years here. ☞

3
Two-Minute Drill

*This activity provides silly fun for younger kids. The goal is
for the players to arrive at a specified point in as close to 2
minutes as possible without using any time-keeping device.
You may be surprised at how long 2 minutes actually is*

Ages: 4 and up

Number of participants: 2 or more

You'll need:
- watch or cell phone with stopwatch
- towel

How to Play:
- Choose a referee and give him the stopwatch.

- The referee draws a starting line in the sand for the players
  to stand behind, then picks a spot free of obstacles 50 feet
  away from the players and lays the towel on the sand.

- At the top of a minute, the referee yells "Go" and starts the
  clock.

- Each player starts to move—crawl, dance, jog, walk, etc.—
  and tries to time his arrival at exactly two minutes. Players
  may count silently, sing a song, or just trust their internal
  clocks to get their timing accurate.

- The referee determines the winner according to who steps
  on the towel closest (either under or over) to the 2-minute
  mark. The winner becomes the referee and starts a new
  game.

June Cussen

Did you know if you're staying at a beachfront location, you should keep the drapes closed and turn off outside lights at night? This is to ensure that newborn loggerhead turtles will not be confused by the lights on land and will crawl toward the moon and their destiny in the ocean.

4
Which Way Is North?

*You need to do this activity before noon on a
sunny day to get the correct result.*

Ages: 4 and up
Number of participants: any

You'll need:
- driftwood or salt hay
- 2 shells
- watch

How to Play:
- Find a spot in the high, dry, soft sand that gets direct sunlight and will not be disturbed by beach visitors or the tide.

- Comb the beach for a straight piece of driftwood or salt hay about 2 feet long. If there is no driftwood, you can use an umbrella or the lifeguard stand to cast a shadow.

- Scrape a 5-inch-deep hole and stick the driftwood or salt hay straight up in the hole, packing sand around it to make it sturdy.

- Place a shell where the shadow tip falls and note the time.

- In exactly 1 hour, place the second shell where the shadow tip now falls.

- With the sun at your back, place your left foot at the first shell and your right foot at the second shell. Guess what! You are now facing north.

- Extend your right arm straight out from your side to point east and your left arm to point west.

Did you know the magnetic pole flips between the North and South Poles every 300,000 years or so? The evidence is found in the magnetic strips around mid-ocean ridges where underwater volcanoes are constantly forming new basaltic rocks.

5
Tell Time without a Clock

*Because the sun's rays are approximately the same each day,
you can build your own sundial. With luck, your sundial will
stay intact and keep you on time for your entire vacation.*

Ages: 4 and up
Number of participants: any

You'll need:
- driftwood or salt hay
- watch
- permanent marker or nail polish

How to Play:

- Find a spot in the high, dry, soft sand that gets direct sunlight and will not be disturbed by beach visitors or the tide.

- Comb the beach for a straight piece of driftwood or salt hay about 3 feet long.

- Scrape a 5-inch-deep hole and stick the driftwood or salt hay straight up in the hole, packing sand around it to make it sturdy.

- Gather one shell for each hour you will be at the beach. Try to gather ugly or common shells beachcombers will not want to pick up.

- At the top of each hour, place a shell where the shadow tip falls. Write the time on the shell with a permanent marker or nail polish. By day's end, your own personal sundial will be complete.

- When you return to the beach each day, you can tell what time it is by seeing where the shadow falls in relation to the shells you placed earlier.

Did you know if you get a sandspur in your foot, you shouldn't jerk it out? The spur will only get stuck in your fingers. Instead, wrap your fingers around a towel and gently pull the spur out. Another method is to use a key to flick the spur from your foot.

6
Fill the Bucket

*This activity keeps kids busy and teaches both
parents and children a little about life.*

Ages: 4 and up

Number of participants: 2–4

You'll need:
- plastic bucket
- 6-ounce plastic cup
- shells
- sand

How to Play:
- Holding your bucket, tell your children, "We won't stop beachcombing until this bucket is completely full of big seashells."

- When the kids say, "The bucket is full," tell them "Look at the room between the shells. Our bucket isn't really full. Let's finish filling the bucket with smaller shells."

- After they add small shells and say, "It's full now!" you say, "No, it's not." Use the plastic cup to add dry, soft sand, counting the cups the bucket will hold. Shake the bucket as you slowly add the sand to compact it.

- Now when the children say the bucket is full, you say, "I bet not." With the plastic cup add ocean water, counting the cups you add until the water flows over the top.

- With the bucket finally full, empty the mixture onto the sand and help the children fill it up in reverse. Put in the same amount of both water and sand used earlier and then put the smaller shells in the bucket.
- Now try to put the large shells back in. Guess what! They won't all fit back in the bucket.

Did you know it is important to put the big things such as family first? Otherwise, small details (like sand and water) will fill up your time. Use this vacation to reconnect with the people who mean the most to you.

7
Beach Blanket Bingo

This game combines beachcombing and memory skills. You can adjust the difficulty by varying either the number of squares or the number of items.

Ages: 3 and up

Number of participants: 2 or more

You'll need:
- beach towel
- beach debris

How to Play:
- Comb the beach for similar pairs of items such as shells, driftwood, and rocks.

- Separate the items into two different piles: Group 1 and Group 2.

- Use a shell to draw two identical square grids in the sand: Grid 1 and Grid 2. You can use any number of squares for the grids. If the players are very young, a 2-by-2 grid should be sufficient.

- The first player turns away from the grid and doesn't peek while the other players pick items from Group 1 and place one item into each square of Grid 1.

- When the grid is filled in, the first player is allowed to see how the grid is arranged for 10 seconds. Cover Grid 1 with the beach towel.

- The first player must now choose from the items in Group 2 and place them in Grid 2 in the same positions as the items in Grid 1.

- When the first player has placed his items, lift the towel from Grid 1 and award 1 point for each item correctly placed. Tally the score in the sand and have the next player take his turn. After five turns, the player with the highest score wins.

Did you know oceans aren't flat? In fact, because of ocean currents and gravitational anomalies, the water tends to bulge up over seamounts and be lower over sea valleys.

8
Beach Blanket Magic

Have you ever wanted to play a magic trick on the kids? This one requires a little preparation. The magic part is to have a secret accomplice.

Ages: 4 and up
Number of participants: any

You'll need:
- beach towel
- small shell

How to Play:
- Tell your children you have the ability to read their minds and slyly suggest the best test would be to find a small shell they have hidden under a towel.

- Draw a 9-square grid, each square 12 inches across.

- Turn your back to the grid and tell the kids to place the shell in one square, then cover the grid with the towel.

- Turn around and act as if you are reading the children's minds. Steal a glance at your accomplice, who will give away the shell's location by touching a part of his body that corresponds to the square in the grid where the shell is hidden. For example, he can touch his left or right hand, elbow, or shoulder to indicate the outside squares or his belly button, heart, or head for the center squares.

- Do a little hocus-pocus and then amaze the children by picking the correct square.

©Vilainecrevette | Dreamstime.com

Did you know the gumbo-limbo tree found in south Florida is known as the tourist tree? Its red bark perpetually peels off the tree, just like a sunburned tourist.

9
Pass the Shell

In this team race, the players pass the shell in front of their bodies on the way down the line and behind their backs toward the finish line.

Ages: 6 and up

Number of participants: 4 or more

You'll need:
- 2 plastic buckets
- 2 towels
- 20 shells for each team

How to Play:
- Divide the players into two evenly matched teams. Pick a captain for each team as well as a referee.
- Each team gathers twenty shells (each about 2 inches long) and places them in their bucket.
- The team members sit cross-legged in a line, facing each other, with the captain on the right. The captain places his team's bucket of shells on a towel to his right.
- When the referee yells "Go," each captain picks a shell from the bucket with his right hand and passes it to the player on his left, who grabs the shell with his right hand and passes it down the line to the next player's right hand.
- When the last player in the line gets the shell, he transfers it to his left hand and passes it behind his back to the player on his right. This player grabs the shell with his left hand

44

and passes it to the next person.

- When the shell reaches the captain, he places it on the towel, not in the bucket.
- The first team to successfully pass all twenty shells back to the captain is the winner. The referee counts the winning team's shells to ensure they are all there.

Did you know the Gulf Stream in the Atlantic Ocean can transport nearly 4 billion cubic feet of water per second, an amount greater than all of the world's freshwater rivers combined?

II

WATER

If you're a first-time visitor to the Eastern Seaboard, you may be disappointed to discover that the water north of Florida isn't crystal clear. Though clear, blue water is beautiful to look at, in terms of nutrients for life, crystal clear water is a virtual desert. The water off the East Coast, however, is a nursery for marine life.

The water's greenish tint comes from phytoplankton (algae), which, along with zooplankton, are present in great numbers in the water. The many rivers and estuaries flowing into the ocean add detritus (decomposing plants such as salt hay), mineral salts, sand, and river silt to the mix. The surf's constant pounding keeps everything stirred up so the visibility is poor, but you can be sure the marine life is well nourished.

The following games and activities all have something to do with water. Enjoy and stay cool, my friends.

Did you know since industrialized fishing began in the 1950s—with its 50-mile-long fishing lines and bottom-dragging nets—hundreds of millions of tons of ocean life have been destroyed? In fact, more than 90 percent of the ocean's largest fish, such as tuna, sharks, and whales, have been taken from the ocean. To be sure you aren't eating an almost-extinct fish, check out www.montereybayaquarium.org before you go out to eat tonight. You'll find out which fish are abundant and caught in environmentally sustainable ways and which fish are overfished or caught in ways that harm other marine life or the environment.

10
Drip-Drip-Dump

The temperature is high, and everyone's ready to get wet.
Check out this coastal version of Duck-Duck-Goose.

Ages: 3 and up
Number of participants: 6 or more

You'll need:
- 16-ounce plastic cup

How to Play:
- Pick one player, the dripper, to fill the cup with seawater. All other players sit in a circle, facing inward, with their legs crossed.

- Play begins as the dripper walks around the outside of the circle of seated players, pausing behind each player. If he decides to drip on the seated player, he pours a drop from the cup and says "Drip." (To keep the salty water from players' eyes, pour the water on the back of the players' heads or necks.)

- At some point, the dripper yells "Dump" and pours the entire cup of water on the back of a player's head. Now the chase begins!

- The person who was dumped on, the dumpee, jumps up and chases the dripper around the circle, trying to tag him before he sits completely down in the dumpee's vacated spot.

- If the dripper sits down before being tagged by the dumpee, the dumpee becomes the dripper. If not, the original dripper tries again.

- If there is a dispute or a close call, the other players serve as judges.

Did you know the largest mountain range on Earth wasn't discovered until the 1950s? That's because most of the 40,000-mile-long Mid-Ocean Ridge is located beneath the ocean.

11
Ping-Pong Ball Race

The goal of this game is to build a canal for a table tennis ball to race up the beach past the finish line.

Ages: 6 and up
Number of participants: 2 or more

You'll need:
- shell for each player
- Ping-Pong ball for each team

How to Play:
- Select evenly matched teams and a referee.

- The players wait in the surf while the referee draws the finish line on the beach about 15 feet away from the players.

- When the referee yells "Go," the players begin to dig a canal with their shells to a depth they think will keep the ball in the canal.

- When their canal is finished, the players drop their balls into it where the water enters the canal. Hint: It helps to dig a small retaining pool in the canal. The water the pool collects stays within the canal, making the next wave to come in have more volume.

- If a wave washes the ball out of the canal before it passes the finish line, the players must start over where the water enters the canal. It's OK for the players to make the canal deeper as the game progresses.

- The first ball to pass the finish line while remaining in the canal is the winner.

- Remember to fill in the canals when you're finished.

Did you know on the television show *MythBusters* (Episode 21), they actually raised a sunken boat with 27,000 table tennis balls? 〜

12
Private Tidal Pool

Tidal pools offer a safe place for children to get wet and play away from the pounding waves. If you can't find a tidal pool, it's as simple as digging a hole to build your own. As you dig the hole, note the alternating layers of dark and light sand on the sides of the hole. The darker layers are magnetite and other heavy minerals washed onto the beach by earlier storms. The lighter layers are sand brought back to the beach when the normal waves returned.

Ages: 3 and up
Number of participants: any

You'll need:
- tide chart
- beach debris
- sand shovel (optional)

Consult a tide chart before you go to the beach as this activity is best done with a falling tide.

How to Play:
- In the damp sand just above the incoming waves, use a shell to dig a shallow hole. Place the sand and salt hay around the hole's edge to warn other beach visitors about the hole.

- Incoming rogue waves, as well as water draining from the porous sand above the hole, will keep the pool full of water for quite a while. (But be aware that the water will get hotter and saltier in time.)

- Make the tidal pool more natural by adding beach debris such as salt hay, shells, and rocks. Be respectful of life, however, and don't place any live creatures in the pool.

- Remember to fill in the hole when you leave to protect other beach visitors and baby loggerhead turtles.

Did you know at Hot Water Beach in New Zealand, you can dig your own hot-water spa? Geothermal springs in the area feed 147° water to the surface at low tide. ✍

13
Drizzle Castle

Reach an almost Zen-like coastal state of mind
while building a beautiful castle.

Ages: 2 and up
Number of participants: any

You'll need:
- tide chart
- beach debris

How to Play:
- In the damp tidal sand with a falling tide, dig a shallow hole. The water draining from the sand above will fill the hole with water.

- Use the sand you removed from the hole to form a base around the outside.

- To begin your first tower, grab a handful of sand from below the water and hold the mixture in your fist. Over the castle base, let the sand and water mixture flow slowly out the bottom of your fist, letting your pinkie finger control the flow. Hold your hand steady as you let the mixture drip onto the previous drips, forming your first tower.

- Another method to drizzle is to point your fingers downward and let the water-laden sand drip slowly from your fingertips.

- Don't worry if a few towers fall over. You will get much better with practice.
- With the castle complete, decorate your castle by using salt hay as flags, shells as windows, etc.
- Remember to fill in any holes you created when you're finished.

Did you know not just oysters but many mollusks can create pearls? In fact, the Caribbean conch will occasionally form a very valuable pink pearl.

14
Saltwater Race

While speed is important, the fastest team does not necessarily win this race. It is more important to bring a full cup of water back from the ocean than one only partially filled.

Ages: 6 and up
Number of participants: 2 or more

You'll need:
- small plastic cup for each team
- plastic bucket for each team

How to Play:
- Away from other beach visitors, find an area with a clear pathway to the ocean.

- Pick evenly matched teams and select a referee.

- Each team places its bucket on a level spot 30 feet from the water's edge. The players line up single file behind the bucket.

- When the players are ready, the referee yells "Go." The first player for each team runs with the plastic cup to the ocean to fill it with seawater. This player then runs back to his bucket, taking care not to spill the water. He empties his water into the bucket and hands the cup to the next player in line, who repeats the process. The first player then takes his place at the back of line.

- The referee keeps an eye on the buckets and determines which team is the first to fill its bucket completely.

Did you know, according to the National Park Service, the highest point in Texas, the Guadalupe Mountains, originated as a marine reef during the Permian period, about 280 to 250 million years ago? There are thousands of seashells embedded in the rocks on the mountaintops.

15
Will It Float?

For an impromptu experiment in buoyancy, gather an assortment of beach debris to see what will and will not float. Keep in mind that the density of tap water is 1.0, while salt water with 3.5 percent dissolved salts has a density of 1.025. The added density allows an item that wouldn't ordinarily float in tap water to float in seawater. (This is a good time to see if the floating sunglass straps you bought really float!)

Ages: 2 and up
Number of participants: any

You'll need:
- plastic bucket
- seawater
- beach debris

How to Play:
- Fill the bucket with seawater. Search the wrack lines and gather an assortment of natural debris such as driftwood, salt hay, shells, and pieces of crab shells. (Remember, there is often another storm-surge wrack line in the dry sand as well.)

- Draw a small grid in the hard sand with a column for each player. At the top of each column, write the player's initials.

- Before you place each item in the bucket, let each player hold the item and ask him or her, "Will it float or sink?"

- Gently place each item on the surface of the water to allow the water's surface tension to help the item float. Observe the results. Give each player a tally mark under his initials for each correct guess.

- When you're finished testing all of the items, add up the tally marks to decide the winner.

Siesta Key Beach, Florida

Did you know because of long-shore drift, the whitest, softest, and coolest sand on Earth is found on Siesta Beach, Florida? Sand granules washed down from southern Appalachian Mountains over millions of years settled around Siesta Key, forming this 99-percent-pure quartz beach.

16
Tip of the Iceberg

This activity turns a science project into a toy that younger kids really enjoy playing with. You'll need to plan ahead by freezing water the day before you go to the beach.

Ages: 2–5

Number of participants: any

You'll need:
- empty 2-liter bottle
- food coloring
- freezer
- knife

How to Play:
- Fill a 2-liter bottle three-fourths full with tap water. Add a few drops of food coloring to make the ice more visible. Stand the bottle upright in the freezer so the ice retains the bottle's round shape. (If you're confident the water won't spill overnight, it's easier to cut the bottle lip off before you fill it with water.)

- Once the water is frozen, carefully cut the bottle from the ice with a knife or scissors. Place the ice in a cooler and take it with you to a tidal pool.

- Drop the ice into the water and observe how it bobs up and down. Because ice is only 90 percent as dense as salt water,

10 percent of the ice will float above the water line. This helps to explain the term "tip of the iceberg."

- As the ice starts to melt, the round shape makes it fun for kids to roll it around, picking up sand and small shells. Just think of the mess as sand art.

Did you know in 1926 an iceberg got as far south as 30° 20' N, 62° 32' W, only 150 nautical miles from Bermuda?

17
Where Did Our Stuff Go?

Have you ever been in the ocean for a long time and when you glance back toward the shore, nothing looks familiar? This activity is best done on a very windy day. The goal is to give children a visual demonstration of the effect that the process known as long-shore drift has on sand and sediment.

Ages: 6 and up
Number of participants: any

You'll need:
- beach ball
- 6 pieces of salt hay

How to Play:

- Walk straight down to the ocean from where your belongings are on the beach.

- Place the first piece of salt hay where you are standing, and toss the ball into the face of a breaking wave. When the ball washes onto the sand, mark the new location with salt hay.

- Continue to toss the ball into the waves and mark its location each time until you have placed all six pieces of salt hay on the sand.

- Because waves break at an angle relative to the shore, you should be able to discern a definite pattern in the salt hay. This same wave action also works on the individual grains of sand in the surf zone, creating what is known as long-

shore drift. (On the southeastern coast of the United States, the effect is usually in a southerly direction.) And, by the way, each time your feet leave the sandy bottom, your body is propelled by the power of the waves down the beach a little bit at a time.

- Remember to take the ball home and remove the salt hay.

Did you know the Dead Sea has a salt content around 33 percent? The water is so dense it is possible to read a book while floating on your back without a float.

III

EARTH

Earth has been in a constant state of change since it was formed 4.5 or so billions of years ago. Even now, 7 major and many minor tectonic plates are floating around Earth, creating earthquakes, mountains, and volcanoes. The sea floor continues to spread, and the continents are constantly on the move.

Climatic change is altering ocean levels even now. In fact, chances are good your vacation is taking place on one of the 405 barrier islands wrapping the United States like a pearl necklace. There are conflicting opinions on how the islands formed, but most developed within the last 5,000 or so years. Each of the following activities has something to do with learning about the coastal environment.

Did you know because of sea floor spreading and subduction zones, the oldest rocks and fossils found in the ocean are less than 200 million years old? Contrast this to the 4.28-billion-year-old rocks at the Nuvvuagittuq greenstone belt in northern Quebec. When tectonic plates collide, the heavier ocean floor subsides beneath the thicker and more buoyant continental crust.

18
The Sand Beneath Your Feet

You may be surprised to see what a rich mixture the sand beneath your feet really is. Grain size is larger near the water and smaller as you go up the beach slope. Sand is actually a combination of many different items. Three distinct colors are present in gray sand—black, brown, and white. White granules are often quartz, feldspar, or shells. Brown granules can also be iron-oxidized quartz, rocks, or shells. The black specks could be detritus, fossils such as sharks' teeth, or shells, magnetite, or ilmenite. If you see a sparkle of light reflected from the sand, it's probably a mica flake.

Ages: 6 and up
Number of participants: any

You'll need:
- sand
- magazine
- magnifying glass
- saucer
- white vinegar
- magnet

How to Play:
- Grab a pinch of sand from the water's edge and sprinkle it on both light- and dark-colored pages of the magazine.

With the magnifying glass, notice the many different colors and sizes of the individual grains. Repeat this process with sand from the middle of the beach and near the dunes.

- Place some sand in the saucer and add a little white vinegar. If the mixture bubbles, it means shell remnants are in the sand. The bubbles are carbon dioxide (like a soft drink) being released as a result of a chemical reaction between the vinegar and the calcium in the shells.

- Place the magnet in the sand to see if it picks up any magnetite molecules.

© Iancucristi | Dreamstime.com

Did you know quartz crystals actually dissipate heat? This is why you can walk on the 99-percent-quartz beach at Siesta Key, Florida, without burning your feet. ❧

19
Saturate the Sand

Here's a simple way to explore how sand and water mix.

Ages: 4 and up
Number of participants: any

You'll need:
- shell with ridges
- plastic bucket
- plastic cup

How to Play:
- Fill the bucket halfway with dry sand. Tilt the bucket back and forth and observe how the sand granules flow over each other. Press the shell into the sand, remove it, and notice how the sand is displaced but no distinct impression is made.

- Pour enough seawater into the bucket to create a sticky solution. Press the shell into the mixture, remove it, and notice the clear impression the shell makes.

- Add water to the bucket to the top of the sand. Press the shell into the sand and notice once again that the shell no longer makes a clear impression.

This is why the ratio of water to sand is important when you're building a sand castle. With no water, the sand granules will simply slide over each other. The sand saturated with water would flow down the castle like a soupy mess, but when the water mixture is correct, the sand granules will stick together to help build a strong sand castle.

© Jaypeteren | Dreamstime.com

Did you know there are two British cemeteries on the Outer Banks of North Carolina? They are the final resting places for British sailors who were on ships sunk by German U-boats at the beginning of World War II.

20
Sand Town

*If you don't have enough time to build a big sand castle,
you can create a small town in a few minutes.*

Ages: 2 and up

Number of participants: any

You'll need:
- plastic cup
- beach debris

How to Play:

- In the damp tidal sand, use a shell to draw two parallel, 5-foot-long lines about 12 inches apart to represent Main Street.

- Pack the plastic cup with damp sand and quickly turn it upside down to dump the sand along the outside edge of one line. Mold the sand with your hands to make it resemble a building. Place about ten buildings on each side of Main Street.

- Draw some side streets. Let children name the streets after their friends or favorite movie characters, and write those names in the sand.

- Use beach debris to decorate the town. Place small shells on the buildings for windows, salt hay for telephone poles, and seaweed strands for electrical lines Be creative!

- To give the town a lived-in feeling, place larger shells on the streets to represent cars, and stand spiral shells in the sand to symbolize people.

- Remember to knock down the structures and to fill in any holes you created. Just like a hurricane, the next incoming tide will smooth the area out.

Did you know the most populated village on the Outer Banks of North Carolina in the late 1800s no longer exists? Diamond City was once the center of the North Carolina whaling industry, but after repeated flooding and a hurricane in 1899, the residents loaded their homes on rafts and abandoned the village. In fact, some of the houses can still be found in Morehead City, North Carolina.

21
Sort the Shells

This activity for younger kids helps them to recognize the difference between similar and dissimilar items and to group like items together.

Ages: 2 and up
Number of participants: any

You'll need:
- beach debris
- plastic bucket

How to Play:
- Take your time to explore the beach with kids as they gather interesting natural debris such as rocks, salt hay, shells, and other items.

- Draw a few 12-inch-square grids and help kids sort the items. Have them place one of each dissimilar item in its own square, sorting by color, shape, size, texture, or other means. If you need more squares, simply add on to the grid.

- Have kids place the remaining items in the appropriate squares with like items. There are no wrong answers. If they think a clamshell belongs in the whelk pile, ask them to explain why. Their reasoning, such as "They are both full of holes," may surprise you. (When you find a shell riddled with little holes, a boring sponge probably attacked the creature inside.)

- With all of the items placed, see if kids can tell by sight which square contains the most items, the least, the biggest, and the prettiest. This is a great time to practice counting skills as well.

- As long as you used natural items, you can leave them alone. The next high tide will clean up the mess.

Did you know mollusks such as oysters and clams form their shells by filtering seawater? They do this by absorbing calcium, carbonate, and other mineral salts from the water they suck in.

22
Walk on the Wild Side

After dinner, don't hit the couch! Grab a flashlight and take a walk on the beach. (Be respectful with your flashlight; don't shine the light on other people or turtles!)

Ages: 4 and up
Number of participants: any

You'll need:
- flashlight with red lens

How to Play:
- As you cross over the boardwalk, shine your flashlight on the sea oats. You may see the federally endangered beach mouse munching on seeds from sea oats and grass while trying to avoid the owls hunting for him from above. On many conservation-minded islands, such as Hilton Head, South Carolina, you may also see deer feeding on sea oats and flowers.

- Shine your light toward the wrack line to see if you can spot a ghost crab searching for a meal. He often scurries back and forth to the ocean to wet his gills under the cover of darkness. You may see sand fleas feeding on wrack line debris as well.

- You may see marine life trapped in tidal pools from the last high tide. Don't be surprised if you see a masked stranger as well: Raccoons often hunt for their next meal in tidal pools.

- Walk into the water ankle deep and kick your feet. You may be surprised to see the water turn fluorescent green, caused by bioluminescent dinoflagellates you've stirred up. Don't venture farther out into the water, though. Skates, small sharks, and squid often come into the shallow water at night to feed.

© Natakuzmina | Dreamstime.com

© Fbxx71 | Dreamstime.com

Did you know a mixture of canola oil and sand will remove a tar ball mess from your feet?

23

Scavenger Hunt

This scavenger hunt helps children learn about what inhabits their beach.

Ages: 6 and up
Number of participants: any

You'll need:
- shell identification guide
- shells
- beach debris
- pencil and paper for each team
- plastic bucket for each team
- watch

How to Play:
- Visit a bookstore or the local beach shop to find names and pictures of shells commonly found at the beach you're visiting.

- Comb the beach with children to pick up different shells, such as oyster, pin, and cockle, as well as other natural beach debris like coral.

- Before you begin play, pass the objects around to the players and let everyone learn the names of the different shells. If you don't know the proper name of an item, at least have everyone agree on what to call it, such as "the small brown shell with a swirl."

- Select evenly matched teams and a referee.

- The referee fills out an identical scavenger hunt list for each team. He should include the smallest complete shell, such as an angel's wing or a spiral shell. He can also list some silly items particular to the beach, such as small drink umbrellas.

- The referee sets a 15-minute time limit and sends the teams off to find the items on their lists.

- When time is up, the referee calls the teams in and uses the list to check the items each team has gathered. The team with the most correct items is the winner. If there is a tie, the referee may use the smallest complete shell as the tiebreaker.

Did you know you should never pick up dead palmetto or palm fronds, especially if they are in a pile? Snakes like to chill out underneath the leaves.

24
Beach Alphabet

This game requires a little at-home preparation and will help young children learn their alphabet and the importance of teamwork.

Ages: 3 and up

Number of participants: 2 or more

You'll need:
- prepared sheet of paper for each team
- pen or pencil for each team
- magazine or clipboard
- watch

How to Play:

- Before going to the beach, write the alphabet on a blank sheet of paper, one letter per line. Make enough copies for each team and for additional games if you wish.

- Go to a designated spot such as the lifeguard stand. Select teams and a referee. It's a good idea to have an adult on each team to serve as the leader and to write observations.

- Each team hunts for one item starting with each letter. To add to the game's difficulty, players must complete the list in alphabetical order. Some examples are "airplane," "dog," "quartz," and "sand." Players may use colors or patterns for harder letters—"red" or "zebra bikini," for example.

- After 15 minutes or so, the referee yells, "Time," and the teams return to the designated spot.

- The referee marks each correct answer with a check mark and ensures that no inappropriate items were listed, such as "dinosaur" or "monkey." The team with the most check marks is the winner.

> Did you know a shipworm is actually a wood-eating clam?

25
Indian Kickball

If you have a large group of kids to entertain, give this game a try. It emphasizes coordination as well as teamwork. The goal is for players to use only their feet to kick a tennis ball around a marked course.

Ages: 7 and up

Number of participants: 4–16

You'll need:
- permanent marker
- tennis ball for each team
- cooler
- beach chair
- 2 towels

How to Play:
- Select evenly matched teams and a referee.

- With the marker, write a number or symbol on a tennis ball for each team.

- Away from other beach visitors, set up a 100-yard course in a zigzag pattern with two obstacles to navigate around. For example, draw the starting line in the tidal sand, walk down the beach 50 yards, and place a cooler on the sand. Draw a right turn arrow in the sand. Walk 25 yards and draw another a right turn arrow around a chair placed in the soft sand. Draw the finish line between two towels 25 yards beyond the chair.

- When the teams are ready, the referee yells, "Go." The teams begin to kick their balls around the course. No player can kick the ball twice in a row. If this occurs, the referee stops the action and makes the guilty team return to the previous obstacle.

- The first team to kick the ball over the finish line is the winner.

Did you know Native Americans started building their Spanish Mount shell midden on Edisto Island, South Carolina, about 4,000 years ago?

IV

WIND

Have you noticed the wind is constantly blowing at the beach? If you're very observant, you've also noticed that, just like clockwork, the wind blows in from the ocean during the day and from the shore at night. The reason is simple: hot air rises. During the day, the sun rapidly warms the air above the landmass. This warm air rises and moves over the more constant, cooler air coming from the ocean, allowing the ocean breeze to dominate the winds. At night this trend reverses as the air above the landmass cools. The now warmer ocean air flows up and over the cooler air from the landmass, allowing the wind to blow from the land toward the ocean.

The constantly blowing wind is a factor in how games are played at the beach. The following games were designed to take advantage of the wind or to be played in spite of it.

Did you know both eagles and ospreys can be seen soaring on wind currents in coastal areas? While many people confuse the two birds, it's actually easy to tell them apart. The osprey is smaller than the eagle and has brown wings and a white underbody; the eagle's body is completely brown. In addition, the osprey will dive underneath the water to catch fish, but the eagle won't.

26
Ring Toss

*The coastal wind has a big impact on this adaptation
of an old-time carnival game. Like horseshoes, the
goal is to throw ringers to beat the competition.*

Ages: 6 and up

Number of participants: 2–4

You'll need:
- scissors
- 3 round, plastic food lids
- driftwood of salt hay

How to Play:
- Use scissors to cut out the center of three plastic lids to the edges, or buy flying disks at the beach store.

- Comb the beach for a piece of driftwood or a sturdy piece of salt hay about 3 feet long. Scrape a 6-inch-deep hole in the soft sand and stand the driftwood as straight as possible in the hole. Refill the hole with packed sand. Draw an 18-inch square around the driftwood to serve as the 1-point scoring area.

- Sprinkle a few grains of sand from your hand to determine the wind direction.

- With the wind at your back, draw a line 10 feet away from the driftwood. The strength of the wind or the players' skill levels may make it necessary to shorten the distance.

- The first player stands behind the line and tosses the 3 disks at the driftwood. The scoring is as follows:
  - A ringer = 5 points
  - A disk that leans against the driftwood = 3 points
  - A disk that lands in the square without touching any of the lines = 1 point
- The first player gathers the disks and writes his score in the sand. The second player then takes his turn.
- The player with the highest score after five rounds is the winner.

If the wind makes it hard for players to score points, then randomly stand 10 pieces of salt hay around the larger target. A ringer around one of the smaller targets is worth 2 points while a leaner is worth 1 point.

Did you know, although it's rare, the possibility of a tsunami exists at any time in coastal areas? If you ever see the sea unnaturally recede from the coast, don't go investigate the flopping fish. Gather everyone in your family and immediately run for safety.

27

Sand Darts

Here's a variation on the game of darts.

Ages: 6 and up

Number of participants: 2 or more

You'll need:
- 3 shells or pieces of coral for each player

How to Play:
- Each player combs the beach for three heavy shells or pieces of coral to use as his darts.

- In the tidal sand, use a shell to draw a circle approximately 12 feet in diameter with a 2-foot bull's-eye in the center.

- Draw 10 lines radiating from the outer edge of the bull's-eye to the outer edge of the circle, and randomly number each pie-shaped segment with the numbers 1 through 10. (You can also write the numbers on small seashells and place them in the segments.)

- Draw a 3-foot-long line approximately 20 feet away from the bull's-eye (or less, depending on the age of the players).

- The first player tries to throw his shells into the segment labeled 1. If he's successful, he then tries for segment 2, and so on. After he has thrown all three shells, the next player takes his turn.

- After a player has successfully landed in all ten segments, he must now land his shell completely within the bull's-eye. The first player to do this is the winner.

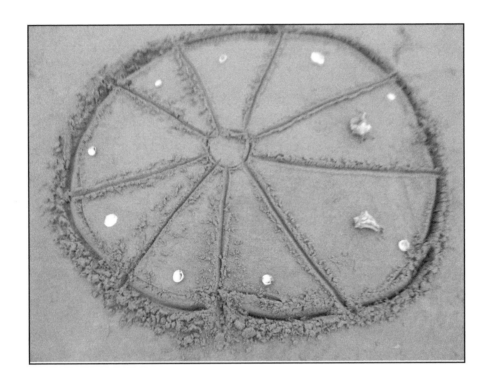

Did you know at the beginning of World War II, the area off the coast of Cape Hatteras, North Carolina, was known as Torpedo Junction? It was the epicenter of German U-boat attacks along the Eastern Seaboard that sank or damaged 259 Allied ships.

28
Edisto Roll

The key to success in this game is to roll a ball with just enough speed through the trench that it stays in the higher scoring zone.

Ages: 6 and up

Number of participants: 2–4

You'll need:
- 3 baseballs
- 7 feet of colored yarn (optional)

How to Play:

- With a sturdy shell in the hard-packed tidal sand, scoop out a 4-foot-square outline about 2 inches deep and 4 inches wide with slopes on 2 sides. Remove this sand from the scoring area. In the square's center, dig a circular hole 8 inches wide by 2 inches deep. Place the displaced sand behind the hole to form a backboard. Stand beach debris in the sand on the back and sides of the scoring area to warn others about the hole. If you have yarn, wrap it around the beach debris to make the area stand out.

- Draw a line 20 feet away from the square.

- The first player rolls his balls one at a time from behind the rolling line toward the scoring area. Scoring is as follows:

  - A ball that lands in the center hole = 5 points
  - A ball that lands on the flat portion within the trench = 3 points
  - A ball that lands in the trench = 1 point

- The first player writes his score in the sand, and the second player takes his turn.

- After five rounds, the player with the highest score is the winner.

- Remember to fill in both the hole and trench and to take the yarn home.

Did you know if you put a small seashell in a glass of vinegar it will be almost gone by week's end? The shell becomes so brittle that you can smash it with just pressure from your fingertips. ✨

29

Bouncy Tennis Basketball

This is the coastal version of the basketball game Around the World.

Ages: 6 and up

Number of participants: 2 or more

You'll need:
- plastic bucket
- 1 tennis ball

How to Play:
- Place the bucket on level, hard-packed tidal sand to serve as the goal. To make the bucket sturdy and to help catch the balls, fill the bucket halfway with dry sand.

- Draw a semicircle 15 feet away from the goal to serve as the shooting line. (Draw a line closer to the goal for younger children.) Starting on the far left, draw five evenly spaced Xs around the semicircle to serve as the spots to bounce from.

- The first player starts on the leftmost X and tries to bounce the tennis ball into the goal. If he makes it, he continues to the next X and tries again. If he misses a shot, he stays on the spot he has advanced to. The next player then takes his turn. Players not shooting should help retrieve the ball.

- The first player to make it all the way to the other end of the semicircle and back—for a total of ten goals—is the winner.

Did you know the term "tsunami" means "harbor wave" in Japanese? When a tsunami wave passed under fishermen in open water, it was barely noticeable, but when the wave reached the harbor, it would rise up and destroy everything it touched.

30
Four Corners of Roll

This is a great game for kids who haven't learned to throw yet. The goal is to be the first to roll the ball into the hole from all four corners.

Ages: 4 and up
Players: 2 to 6

You'll need:
- baseball

How to Play:
- In the high, dry tidal sand, draw a 30-foot square. In each corner draw an 18-inch quarter circle. Mark the corners with the numbers 1 through 4 in order.
- In the center of the square, dig a hole 8 inches in diameter and 2 inches deep. Remove the dug-up sand from the rolling area.
- Play Rock-Paper-Scissors to determine the rolling order.
- The first player stands in corner 1 and attempts to roll the ball into the hole. If he succeeds, he continues to move around the corners until he misses. He stays on the corner he has advanced to. Then the next player takes his turn. Players waiting for their turns may help retrieve the balls.
- The first player to roll the ball into the hole from all four corners is the winner.
- Remember to fill in the holes when you're finished.

- A variation is for players to stand in the center of the square and roll the ball to holes dug in the corners.

Did you know in Charleston, South Carolina, the intersection of Meeting and Broad Streets is known as the Four Corners of Law? St. Michael's Church represents God's law, a post office represents federal law, a courthouse represents state law, and city hall represents local law.

31

First to Fifty

Use this game to sharpen kids' tossing and counting skills.

Ages: 8 and up

Number of participants: 2

You'll need:
- 5 shells for each player

How to Play:
- Each player combs the beach for five shells different from those of his opponent.

- In the high, dry tidal sand, draw a 4-foot-wide by 15-foot-long rectangle. At one end of the rectangle, with the wind at your back, draw a line 2 feet from and parallel to the rectangle's boundary to toss from.

- At the other end of the rectangle, draw a line 2 feet from and parallel to the rectangle's boundary. Draw another line 2 feet closer to the tossing line, then another 2 feet closer than the previous one. Draw two intersecting lines across the lines you just drew to form a 3-by-3 grid.

- Write 1, 2, and 3 in the three boxes closest to the tossing line; 4, 5, and 6 in the boxes in the next row; and 7, 8, and 9 in the boxes in the last row.

- Players take turns tossing their shells one at time toward the scoring area. A shell touching a boundary line doesn't count.

- After the first round of shells has been thrown, each player adds up his score.

- Players continue to alternate turns until one player reaches 50 points. If this player threw first, the second player is allowed one more throw to try to beat the first player's score.

Did you know a group of small holes in the tidal sand surrounded by "chocolate sprinkles," or fecal pellets, is the home of a mud shrimp? He is usually buried about 18 inches beneath the sand. ✍

32
Ribbon Dancing

In this 2,000-year-old Chinese folk dance, the ribbons symbolize the clouds. Dancers hope to make the gods happy so they will send the rain needed for a bountiful crop.

Ages: 3 and up

Number of participants: any

You'll need:
- 3/8-inch-diameter, 12-inch-long wood dowels
- brightly colored ribbons
- rubber bands

How to Play:

It's best to make the ribbon wands at home and take them to the beach with you. Each child's ribbon length should be at least as long as that child is tall. There are many ways to attach the ribbon to the wooden dowels. One of the easiest is to split the end of the dowel. Slide a few strands of ribbon into the split, wrap the ribbon around the dowel a few times, and secure the ribbon with a rubber band.

- Teach kids to move their wands up and down, sideways, over their heads, and trailing behind them as they run or walk backwards.
- Don't forget to have kids bow at the end of each dance.
- Bring a couple of extra ribbon wands to share with your newly found beach friends.

> **Did you know if your daughter becomes very good at ribbon dancing, she could be an Olympic athlete? Ribbon dancing is actually an Olympic sport!**

V

LOW TIDE

If the world were one giant ocean, it would have two equal high and low tides a day as the gravitational pull of both the moon and the sun affected the Earth. But with continents and ocean currents such as the Gulf Stream getting involved, it gets a little more complicated.

There are three main types of tides on Earth. In the United States the Eastern Seaboard experiences what are known as semidiurnal tides, meaning there are two roughly equal high and low tides each lunar day. A lunar day equals 24 hours 50 minutes, so the tides change about every 6 hours 12 minutes. This explains why high and low tides occur 50 minutes later each successive day. The West Coast has mixed semidiurnal tides, meaning there are two high and low tides of unequal height. The Gulf Coast typically has a diurnal tide, meaning it has only one high tide and one low tide per day.

Periods of low tide offer the widest beach to spread out and play. The following games make use of the wide tidal beach.

Did you know Morecambe Bay in the United Kingdom can experience a tidal range of **35** feet during spring tides? Because of the bay's shallow, sloping nature, the sea can ebb as far as **7** miles from the high-tide mark.

33
Folly Field Roll

The whole family can enjoy this simple and competitive game for hours. Changing the goal size varies the skill level, making this game suitable for all ages.

Ages: 6 and up
Number of participants: 2–4

You'll need:
- driftwood or salt hay
- baseball

How to Play:
- In the flatter, dry tidal sand away from water, use a shell to draw a 30-foot-long-by-10-foot-wide rectangular playing field. In each corner, place driftwood or other debris to mark the boundaries, which also serve as the rolling lines.

- At each end of the field, dig a semicircular hole 10 inches long by 4 inches wide and 2 inches deep to serve as the goal. Use the sand from the hole to form a backboard to help hold the ball in the goal. Remember to mark behind the hole with salt hay.

- Players stand at opposite ends of the field. The first player stands behind his boundary line and attempts to roll the ball into the goal at the opposite end of the field. The second player then picks up the ball and tries to make a goal at the opposite end. A ball landing in the goal is worth 1 point.

- Players are not allowed to interfere with their opponents' ball while it is rolling.

- After ten rolls, players switch sides. The first player to reach 10 points wins the game. If no one scores after ten rolls, increase the goal size.

- Remember to fill in the hole when you're finished.

Did you know both fiddler and ghost crabs hibernate in their holes during the cold weather months? 🐚

34
Baseball Shuffleboard

Here's the popular cruise ship game gone to the beach.

Ages: 6 and up

Number of participants: 2

You'll need:
- 3 baseballs

How to Play:
- In the flatter, dry tidal sand, draw a rectangle 30 feet long by 10 feet wide. At each end, draw the scoring triangle containing areas marked 10, 8, 7, and 10 OFF. Create a ½-inch-deep gully with a ridge around the triangle. It helps to have both the gully and the ridge to keep the ball in the scoring zones.

- The first player stands behind the boundary line at one end of the rectangle, while the other player stands behind the other end. The first player rolls the three balls one at a time toward the other end of the board.

- After the first player rolls three balls, his opponent gathers them up, adds up the first player's scores, and then takes his turn.

- If a ball lands in the 10 OFF area, that player loses 10 points off his score, so it's good strategy to knock that ball out of the box with the next roll.

- As play progresses, it will be necessary to rework the ridges.
- After ten rounds, the player with the higher score is the winner.

35
Coastal Bowling

The only thing missing in this beach game is the automatic ball return feature!

Ages: 4 and up

Number of participants: 2

You'll need:
- driftwood or salt hay
- yarn (optional)
- 3 tennis balls

How to Play:
- In flatter tidal sand, dig ten holes in a triangular pattern with one hole at the tip, two in the next row, three in the next row, and four in the last row, just like the setup at a bowling alley. Make each hole 6 inches in diameter and 2 inches deep with 1 foot between each row.

- Stand driftwood or salt hay around the back and sides of the area to protect other beach visitors from stepping in the holes. String yarn around the markers if you like.

- Draw a rolling line 20 feet away from the first hole.

- The first player rolls three balls one at a time toward the holes, trying to land a ball in one of them. The scoring is as follows:

  - A ball that lands in the single hole = 10 points
  - A ball that lands in the second row = 5 points

- A ball that lands in the third row = 3 points
- A ball that lands in the fourth row = 1 point

- After the first player has rolled all three balls, he adds up his score, and the second player takes his turn.

- The player with the higher score after five rounds is the winner.

- Remember to fill in the holes when you're finished and to take the yarn home.

Did you know the world's largest recorded tidal wave occurred on July 9, 1958, in Lituya Bay, Alaska? An earthquake on the Fairweather Fault set off a huge wave measuring 1,720 feet high. ✍

36
Dots to Boxes

This game stimulates the mind while passing the time.
The object is to complete as many squares as possible.

Ages: 4 and up

Number of participants: 2

You'll need:
- small shells (optional)

How to Play:
- In the tidal sand, draw a grid four squares high by four squares wide to make sixteen squares. Draw sixteen Os or dots 6 inches apart in the squares. You can also use shells instead of dots.

- Players alternate turns drawing a straight line from one O or shell to another, either vertically or horizontally but not diagonally. If a player connects two dots but doesn't complete a square, his turn is over.

- If a player completes a square, he gets another turn. Once his turn is over, he carefully writes his initial in each square he completed before the next player takes his turn.

- Play continues until the entire grid is filled in with initials. The player with more of his initials on the grid is the winner.

Did you know the bottlenose dolphin is not a fish but a mammal that is warm-blooded, breathes air, and feeds its young milk?

37

Capture the Shark

*This game is a variation of Dots to Boxes. In this game,
however, the goal is to keep the hungry shark from biting his
tail by drawing a continuous line without squaring in a box.
The person who is forced to complete a box loses the game.*

Ages: 4 and up

Number of participants: 2–4

You'll need:
- small shells (optional)

How to Play:
- In the tidal sand, draw a grid five squares high by five squares wide. Draw twenty-five Os or dots 6 inches apart. You can also use shells instead of dots.

- Players alternate turns drawing a straight line from one O or shell to another, either vertically or horizontally but not diagonally. If a player connects two dots and completes a square, he loses.

- Use tally marks to keep score in the sand. The first player to win five games wins the match.

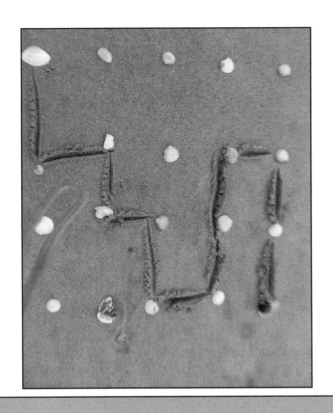

Did you know a shark's teeth are naturally white?
When you're lucky enough to find a black, gray, or
brown shark's tooth, you have a fossil that could be
thousands or even millions of years old.

38
Sand Badminton

Even teenagers will enjoy playing this challenging game.

Ages: 8 and up
Number of participants: 2–3

You'll need:
- tennis ball

How to Play:
- On the hard-packed tidal sand, pick a level spot away from other beach visitors.
- Draw a rectangle 12 feet long by 6 feet wide. Draw a line across the center to create two squares. This line serves as the net.
- One player stands in each square, facing the other. If there is a third player, he serves as the referee, standing at the net line and ruling if shots are fair or foul.
- One player hits the ball with his open palm into his opponent's square. The ball must go over the net line and bounce inside the boundary lines. Otherwise, it is a loss of serve.
- If the ball bounces within the receiver's square, the players volley, hitting the ball back and forth to each other. Play continues until one player fails to hit the ball back over the net line, hits the ball out of bounds, or lets the ball go past him.

- Only the server can score points. If the receiver loses the volley, the server earns 1 point. If the server loses the volley, the receiver gets to serve.

- A player must win by 2 points. The first player to score 11 points or more with a 2-point lead is the winner. The loser and the referee now switch places.

Did you know the largest whirlpool in the Western Hemisphere is the Old Sow Whirlpool located between Deer Island, New Brunswick, Canada, and Moose Island, Eastport, Maine?

39
Whales and Minnows

*This circular tag game keeps everyone in a contained
area away from your beach neighbors.*

Ages: 6 and up
Number of participants: 6 or more

How to Play:

- In the tidal sand away from other beachgoers, draw a circle 40 feet in diameter as the outer boundary for the game. Draw another circle 3 feet inside the outer boundary to form the outer running lane. At the center of the circle, draw a circle 4 feet in diameter. Now draw four evenly spaced, 3-foot-wide running lanes, radiating from the center circle to the large circle's inner boundary. Your playing field should look like the photo on the next page.

- Choose a player to be the whale, who begins the game standing in the center circle. The other players are the minnows, who can stand anywhere inside the running lanes or the outer circle. Select a referee who will make sure everyone stays within the lines.

- Play begins when the whale moves along the running lanes to tag the minnows. Both whale and minnows can run in any direction, but they must remain inside the running lanes. Minnows can pass each other going in different directions, but they cannot step outside the lines. If a minnow steps outside the lines, he is automatically tagged. Likewise, if the whale runs outside the lines, the tagged minnows become free.

- When a minnow is tagged, he becomes a whale and helps tag the remaining minnows.
- The last minnow to be tagged is the winner and becomes the whale for the next game.

Did you know the largest animal to ever live on Earth is the blue whale? To get an idea of how big the blue whale is, draw a line in the sand and ask an adult to take thirty-five steps down the beach. The distance between the adult and the line is approximately the length of an adult whale.

40
Tic-Tac-Toe

This easy-to-play game is perfect for the beach.

Ages: 4 and up
Number of participants: 2

You'll need:
- 5 shells for each player (optional)

How to Play:
- Draw two vertical and horizontal lines that intersect to form an open grid.
- You can play the traditional way and mark Xs and Os in the sand or play with shells.
- Play Rock-Paper-Scissors to determine which player goes first. Since the player who goes first will win twice as often, it's fair to alternate the player who goes first after each round.
- The first player is X and the second is O. The players take turns placing their markers in unoccupied squares. The first one to get three in a row is the winner.
- If all of the squares get filled in and there is no winner, it's a draw.
- Keep score by tally marks in the sand.

Did you know the eastern oyster can release up to one hundred million eggs during the spawning season in June, July, and August? The bad taste of the egg-laden oysters, along with a lack of refrigeration, led to the old wives' tale that the oysters aren't safe to eat in months that don't have an R in them.

41
Expanded Tic-Tac-Toe

If your usual tic-tac-toe game keeps ending in a tie, it's time to trade up to a larger grid, which changes the game's dynamics. Just getting three in a row doesn't win this game, though. The game isn't over until there's a marker in every empty square.

Ages: 4 and up
Number of participants: 2

You'll need:
- 14 shells for each player

How to Play:
- In the tidal sand, draw four intersecting vertical and horizontal lines to make twenty-five squares.

- Play Rock-Paper-Scissors to determine which player goes first. Players take turns placing their shells in empty squares to get three, four, or even five in a row in any direction. Remember to alternate who goes first with each new round.

- Once every square has a shell in it, it's time to add up the scores as follows:
    - Five in a row = 5 points
    - Four in a row = 3 points
    - Three in a row = 1 point
- Each marker can be counted multiple times. The player with the higher score is the winner.

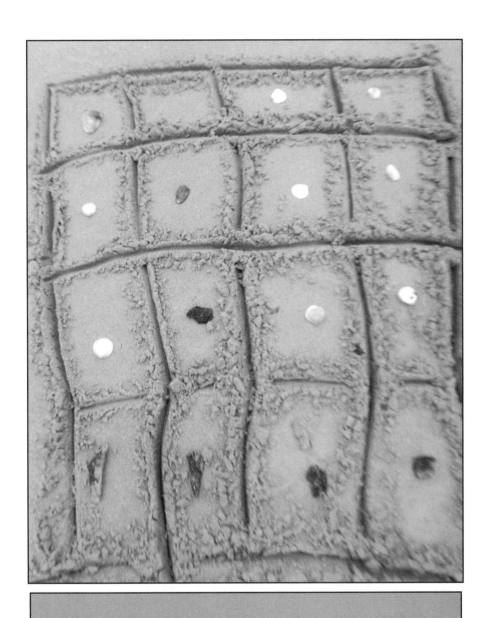

Did you know the state of Maine has more than 2,000 islands and 63 lighthouses? But with well over 100 working lighthouses, the inland state of Michigan holds the record for the most beacons. ✍

42
Three in a Row

This is the thinking person's version of tic-tac-toe with a little checkers thrown in.

Ages: 6 and up

Number of participants: 2

You'll need:
- 3 shells for each player

How to Play:

- In the tidal sand, draw a nine-square grid large enough to hold the shells the players selected. The players sit on opposite sides of the grid.

- Each player places his three shells along the row closest to him, leaving the middle row vacant.

- Play Rock-Paper-Scissors to determine which player goes first. Remember to alternate who goes first with each new round.

- Each player takes turns moving his shells into an empty space, which doesn't have to be an adjacent square; players can jump across the grid to any empty space.

- Play continues until a player gets three shells in a row vertically, horizontally, or diagonally to become the winner. The winning row can't be in the starting position unless each player has had more than five moves.

Did you know the new surfing craze is to surf tidal bores? The incoming ocean tide forms waves that travel upstream into rivers such as the Amazon. Surfers have been able to catch a wave and ride the Amazon tidal bore for many miles inland. ✍

VI

HIGH TIDE

During the Cretaceous period (145 to 65 million years ago), the sea level was approximately 1,100 feet above the present level. Both polar ice caps had melted, and the ocean covered much of Earth for about 60 million years. It was during this ultimate high tide that the epicontinental Western Interior Seaway covered most of western North America from Canada to the Gulf of Mexico. This is the reason sharks' teeth are found in Kansas and hydrocarbon-based oil is plentiful in Texas.

High tides force beach visitors to the backshore. These games and activities take advantage of the dry, fine, soft sand available there.

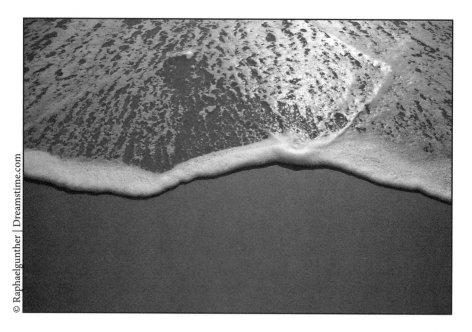

© Raphaelgunther | Dreamstime.com

Did you know you can look at the moon to know the tides? Because the gravitational pulls of both the sun and the moon exert their power over the tides, it makes sense that when they are aligned at both the full moon and new moon stages, the tides will be much higher than normal. This is known as a spring tide because the tides seem to spring up. Neap tides occur when the sun and moon are at right angles to each other, effectively canceling each other's gravitational pull. Neap tide gets its name from the fact the tides are nearly as even as possible.

43
Dizzy Race

You're sure to get more laughs than serious competition in this silly race. The goal of this game is to be the first team to retrieve all of their flip-flops and return them to their base. The catch? Players must make themselves dizzy by spinning around before they take off running.

Ages: 8 and up

Number of participants: an even number

You'll need:
- flip-flop for each player

How to Play:

The dizzy races held between innings at minor league baseball games have each player spin ten times, but this may be too much for younger kids. Experiment with fewer spins, and decide what works best for the players in your group.

- This game is best played in the soft, dry sand away from other beach visitors. Divide into evenly matched teams and select a referee.

- Draw a line for each team to stand behind in single file. Have team members place their flip-flops in their own pile 30 feet away.

- When the referee yells, "Go," the first player for each team lowers his head down to waist level, grabs his nose, and begins spinning around a set number of times, counting out

© Lixun | Dreamstime.com

loud as he completes each turn. He then attempts to run toward his team's pile to pick up a flip-flop and return it to his team. If a player returns another team's flip-flop, it counts for the other team.

- When a player returns to his line, he tags the next player in line, who repeats the process until all the flip-flops have been returned. The first team to do so is the winner.

Did you know Spanish moss is neither Spanish nor moss? It is actually an epiphyte, or air plant, that is a member of the pineapple family. And, no, the plant doesn't harm the host tree. ✎

44
Run for the Flounder

In this circle tag game there are no losers, only winners. Because this game has a unique format, even the smallest children can have fun.

Ages: 4 and up
Number of participants: 6 or more

How to Play:

- Pick one player to be the flounder for the first round.

- The other players form a circle, holding hands with their arms outstretched.

- The flounder walks outside the circle. He stops between two players, pulls their arms apart, and yells, "Run for the flounder!"

- The two players now take off running in opposite directions to race back to the vacant spot. (If a player's left arm was pulled, he runs to the right.)

- The flounder steps into the vacant spot and holds both hands in the air.

- The first player to run around the circle and tag the flounder's raised hand rejoins the circle, while the slower player becomes the flounder for the next round.

Did you know it is much easier to pull a stroller through the soft sand than to push it? ∽

45
Musical Sit-Down

This is a coastal version of musical chairs without the chairs.

Ages: 3 and up

Number of participants: 4 or more

You'll need:
• iPod or radio

How to Play:
• Away from other beach visitors, find the softest, driest sand you can. Draw a deep circle in the sand large enough for the players to dance around. (Adults will find it painfully obvious after a few rounds why you want the softest sand available.)

• Choose a referee, who will also play the music.

• The referee starts a song, and the players begin to dance or walk around the circle.

• At a random point in the song, the referee stops the music. Each player must sit down in the sand as quickly as possible. The last player to be completely seated is eliminated from the game.

• The referee resumes the music, and the players repeat the cycle until only one player remains. The winner becomes the referee for the next round.

Did you know the average sea level on the West Coast of the United States is actually higher than on the East Coast? ✍

46
Nim

The goal of this game is to outwit your opponent so on his last turn there is only one object left for him to pick up. The smart player not only thinks of his future moves but also anticipates what his opponent will do.

Ages: 8 and up

Number of participants: 2

You'll need:
- beach debris

How to Play:

- Gather sixteen shells or pieces of salt hay about 2 inches long and place them in a line in the sand.

- Players alternate taking turns. Each player must remove between one and three objects from the line during each turn.

- Keep score by tally marks in the sand. The first player to win five games wins the match.

Just like Rock-Paper-Scissors, this game is more complicated than it first appears. Perhaps this is why I have never won this game against my wife. Ever.

Did you know those quarter-size holes you see in the dry sand above the tidal line are the homes of ghost crabs? During the day the crabs stay about 18 inches underground in their damp burrows to avoid being eaten by birds.

47
Pick Up the Sticks

This activity can help a child with both manual dexterity and counting skills. The goal is to successfully pick up a piece of salt hay without moving any adjacent pieces.

Ages: 5 and up

Number of participants: 2–3

You'll need:
- 20 pieces of salt hay

How to Play:
- Gather twenty pieces of salt hay between 6 and 10 inches long.

- Determine the playing order, and have the first player hold the salt hay in his hand. He holds his hand 2 to 6 inches above a level place in the tidal sand and opens his hand, allowing the pieces to fall in a random pile. The closer the pieces are to the sand when dropped, the closer they will stay together. Conversely, the farther away they are when dropped, the more the pieces will scatter, making them easier to pick up without penalty.

- The first player attempts to pull a piece from the pile without disturbing or moving any piece other than the one he's trying to pick up. The other players act as judges to determine whether another piece is moved.

- Each player is allowed one attempt per turn to pick up a piece. If he is successful he places the piece in his pile.

- Players continue alternating turns until the last piece is picked up.

- The player with the most pieces is the winner.

Did you know the lower Florida Keys are built on ancient coral reefs? Residents must import clay from Georgia to build their baseball fields. Just imagine sliding into second base on a bed of coral. Ouch!

48
Pickle (a.k.a. Rundown)

The goal of this game is for the base runner to reach a base without being tagged while staying within the baseline. The base guard's goal is to tag the runner out.

Ages: 6 and up

Number of participants: 3

You'll need:
- sand sock (see Beach Lingo) or tennis ball
- 2 towels

How to Play:

- In the soft sand, far away from other beach visitors, place two towels 60 feet apart to serve as bases. Designate one as first base, the other as second base.

- To keep players from running all over the beach, define the baseline by drawing two parallel lines 8 feet apart from first base to second.

- Designate one player to be the base runner, who takes his position between the two bases. Another player guards first base while the third guards second base. The first baseman, with the ball in hand, approaches the runner to tag him out, forcing the runner toward the second baseman. The guards chase the base runner and toss the ball back and forth to each other in an attempt to tag the base runner before he safely reaches a base.

- Play continues until the runner is tagged, runs outside the baseline, or makes it safely to a base, which earns him 1 point.

- Players take turns being the runner. The first player to score 5 points wins.

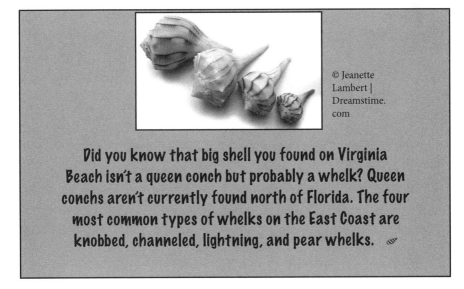

© Jeanette Lambert | Dreamstime.com

Did you know that big shell you found on Virginia Beach isn't a queen conch but probably a whelk? Queen conchs aren't currently found north of Florida. The four most common types of whelks on the East Coast are knobbed, channeled, lightning, and pear whelks.

49
String Hunt for Treasure

*Who doesn't love a treasure hunt? While this activity takes
a little planning and stealth to set up, it's worth it.*

Ages: 3 to 6
Number of participants: any

You'll need:
- plastic box with lid
- treasure
- 100 feet of string
- treasure note

How to Play:
- Before leaving for the beach, pack the plastic box with treasure such as coins, costume jewelry, and toys. Also place in the box the string and a short pirate note that says something like, "Arrgh! It's your lucky day." Hide the box in the beach bag to take with you to the beach.

- While the children are occupied with another activity, it's time to bury the treasure. Take the box to the dry, soft sand about 50 feet away from the path leading off the beach, and dig a hole 8 inches deep. Remove the pirate note from the box. Wrap the string several times around the box, place the box in the hole, and cover it with sand.

- As you walk toward the boardwalk, lay the string out in a haphazard manner and cover it with sand as you walk.

- At the steps or on the path off the beach, tie the remaining string around the note. Hide the note so other beach visitors will not ruin the surprise.

- As you walk off the beach, point out the note to the kids and tell them to pick it up. Imagine their surprise when they find the string attached. Read the note aloud, and have the kids follow the string to the treasure box.

- Once the treasure has been found, fill in the hole and take everything home with you.

50

X Marks the Spot

*This is an old-fashioned treasure hunt with a
little deception and a map thrown in. Build up the
excitement as you follow the map's directions.*

Ages: 3–5

Number of participants: any

You'll need:
- plastic container with lid
- treasure
- pencil and paper
- small piece of yarn

How to Play:
- Before going to the beach, fill the container with treasure such as candy, marbles, and toys.

- Go to the beach a few minutes before everyone else to hide the treasure. Start from a landmark, such as a pier or lifeguard chair, and count off the steps to the location where you'll bury the container in a shallow hole. To be sure you can find it, mark the spot with a piece of unique beach debris. Draw on the map pirate symbols and the directions such as, "Start at the second pier leg closest to the shore, facing the morning sun. Walk ten steps toward the lifeguard stand, then ten steps to the right, and you will find my treasure tonight." Roll the note up, tie yarn around it, and hide it in your beach bag.

- While the kids are distracted by another activity, pull out the note and act as if it just blew onto your beach towel. Read the note aloud and let kids discover the treasure.

- Remember to fill in the hole and take everything home with you.

Did you know many people believe the Florida pirate Black Caesar buried millions of dollars in treasure around the Florida Keys? So far, none of it has been found, however.

137

51

Treasure Hunt

*This activity lets younger kids do two things they love,
dig in the sand and find treasure. Take the children's ages
into account and avoid items they could choke on.*

Ages: 3–5

Number of participants: any

You'll need:
- beach towel
- treasure
- plastic bucket

How to Play:
- Find a spot in the soft sand above the wrack line and dig a 3-inch-deep indentation a little smaller than the towel. Place the towel in the hole so the edges stick out on all sides.

- Refill the hole with sand, randomly mixing in treasure such as coins, plastic jewelry, and toys. Count the number of items you place in the hole.

- When the hole is full, let the kids enjoy themselves as they dig with their hands in the soft sand to find the treasure. Have them place the treasure in the bucket so it doesn't get lost.

- When it's time to leave, have two people grab the towel edges and pick the towel straight up from the hole. Shake the towel back and forth to locate any treasure hidden in the sand the children didn't find. Count the items to be sure everything was found.

- Remember to fill in the hole and take everything home with you.
- To clean the towel, rinse it off first in the ocean, then again at an outdoor shower before placing it in your washing machine.

Did you know in 1985, treasure hunter Mel Fisher found two wrecked Spanish galleons near Key West, Florida, with a treasure worth an estimated $450 million? If you're in Key West, stop by and visit his museum.

VII

DICE AND
MARBLE GAMES

Oddly enough, every time my family brings out the marbles to play a game, a child will approach us and ask what they are. Marbles have been around an awfully long time. In fact, some early rolled clay balls have been found in prehistoric caves. Dice, on the other hand, are much younger than marbles—more like only 5,000 years old. The oldest six-sided dice were found in China and date to 600 years B.C.

It is best to play a dice game on dry, hard-packed sand. If there is none available, the next best option is to place a towel over an area of sand you have smoothed out with your hands. Because of the natural slope found on beaches, it's usually best to roll marbles straight down the slope rather than across it.

Did you know the coastline of Japan is dotted with tsunami markers? They were placed many years ago to warn future generations about the danger of tsunamis. Some of the markers still standing are more than 600 years old.

52
Seashell Around the Clock

This fast-paced game combines addition skills with the roll of the dice. The goal is to be the first player to move his marker around the clock face by rolling the numbers one through twelve in succession. Using three dice allows the game to move faster.

Ages: 6 and up

Number of participants: 2 or more

You'll need:
- 3 dice
- unique shell for each player

How to Play:
- In the tidal sand, draw a clock face 2 feet in diameter. Place twelve shells around the clock face to mark the hours.
- All players roll one die. The highest roll goes first, the next highest goes second, etc.
- Each player starts with his marker at 12:00 and rolls the dice, hoping to roll the numbers he needs to advance around the clock. A player can use any combination of the numbers he rolls in order to get the numbers he needs. For example, if he rolls a one and a two, he can move to 1:00, then on to 2:00, and then add the dice to move to 3:00. As a player advances around the clock, his ability to add the numbers on the dice will become more important.

- If a player can't advance after his roll, he passes the dice to the next player.

- The first player to move his marker all the way around the clock is the winner.

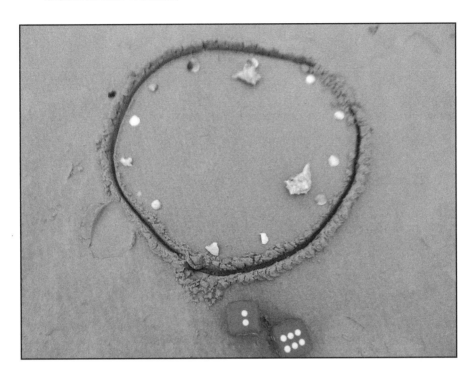

Did you know the sand dunes at Jockey's Ridge State Park in Nags Head, North Carolina, are a great place to look for fulgurites? These are quartz granules fused together by lightning strikes. But don't remove them because the park is a protected natural area. ∾

53

Free the Dolphin

The goal of this game is to free your "dolphins" from the underwater cages they are being held captive in.

Ages: 4 and up

Number of participants: 2–4

You'll need:
- 1 die
- 6 unique shells for each player

How to Play:
- Draw a 12-by-18-inch rectangle in the tidal sand. Within the rectangle draw five vertical lines 3 inches apart. Mark each box with the numbers 1 through 6. These rectangles represent the "cages" where the dolphins are being held captive.

- Each player places his dolphins (shells) in the rectangles marked with the number he hopes to roll. A player can place any number of his six dolphins in any rectangle he chooses.

- Each player rolls the die once per turn. If the rolled number matches a cage holding a dolphin, the player removes his dolphin from the cage.

- The first player to remove all of his dolphins from their cages is the winner.

Did you know at the Dolphin Research Center in Marathon, Florida, you can swim with bottlenose dolphins? But plan ahead: Tickets sell out months in advance. 〰️

54
100-Yard Dash

This game combines the roll of the die with a race, so even the smallest child can win. The goal is to roll high numbers with the dice to cross the finish line first.

Ages: 5 and up

Number of participants: 2 or more

You'll need:
- unique shell for each player
- 1 die for each player

How to Play:
- In the tidal sand away from other beach visitors, use a shell to draw two parallel lines, 25 feet long and 1 foot apart.

- Connect the parallel lines with vertical lines 3 inches apart. When you're finished, the track will resemble a ladder with one hundred rungs.

- Designate one end as the start and the other as the finish. Stand salt hay or draw a large X in the last box to serve as the finish line.

- Players roll their dice to decide who goes first. The highest number wins.

- Taking turns, each player rolls his die and moves his marker the number of spaces shown on the die. Players can occupy the same rectangle without penalty.

- The first player to cross the finish line is the winner. If this player rolled before the others and the race is close, draw out five more boxes. The other players get one more roll to see if they can pass the winner.

Did you know an Atlantic sailfish was once timed covering 100 yards in 3 seconds while leaping? This works out to a speed of 68 miles per hour!

55
Speedway

Lay a track out in the tidal sand and let
"drivers" try out coastal racing.

Ages: 4 and up

Number of participants: 2–6

You'll need:
- 1 unique shell for each player
- 1 die for each player

How to Play:
- Draw an 8-by-10-foot oval to serve as the track's outside boundary. Draw another oval 18 inches inside to serve as the track's inside boundary. Connect the two ovals with lines 12 inches apart. This gives you seven spaces down the straightaway and five spaces in each turn. This also provides a large infield for the players to move around in.

- Designate the start/finish line with a large X in the center space on one straightaway. Outside the oval at the start/ finish line, each player writes his initials in the sand.

- Players place their markers on the start/finish line, take turns rolling their die once, and move their markers the corresponding number of spaces around the track.

- More than one player may occupy the same space without penalty.

- If a player rolls the same number three times in a row, he "spins out." Rather than advancing on the third roll, he must move backwards that number of spaces.

- Players draw a tally mark under their initials each time they pass the start/finish line.

- The first player to complete five laps is the winner.

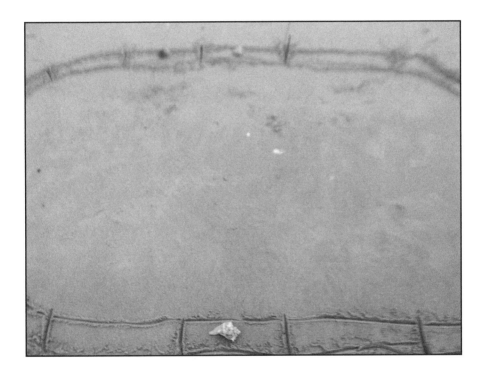

Did you know the original stock car races held in Daytona took place on a stretch of the beach?

56
Dare to Risk It

This dice game forces players to decide when it's time to quit pushing their luck. The catch is anytime a player rolls a 1, his turn is over and any points he has accumulated disappear.

Ages: 8 and up

Number of participants: 2–4

You'll need:
- 1 die

How to Play:

- For truer rolls, play this game on a towel or hard-packed tidal sand.

- Select a scorekeeper, who writes down the result of each roll in the sand and tallies the points earned at the end of each player's turn.

- Each player rolls the die and decides to keep the points accumulated or to continue and risk having a one come up.

- For example; the first player rolls the die four times and gets a 6, a 4, a 5, and a 6 for a total of 21 points, but he pushes on and rolls a 1. This causes him to both lose his turn and the points he has accumulated, for a score of zero.

- The second player rolls his die five times and gets a 4, a 3, a 4, a 5, and a 2 and decides to hold at 18 points. He then hands the die to the next player.

- The first player to reach 100 points is the winner.

Did you know the tallest mountain on Earth—based on height from the base to the top—isn't Mount Everest but Hawaii's Mauna Kea? In fact, with a height above sea level of 13,796 feet and below sea level of 19,700 feet, Mauna Kea has a total height of 33,496 feet, which is about one mile higher than Mount Everest.

57
Poker Dice

When there's too much wind to even think about playing cards on the beach, try this dice game instead. For more consistent rolls, play on the tidal sand or a towel.

Ages: 6 and up

Number of participants: 2–4

You'll need:
- 5 dice for each player

How to Play:
- As in regular draw poker, all players roll their five dice at the same time. Each player sets aside the ones he wants to keep, such as a 6 and a 6, and then rolls the remaining dice. Each player must leave his dice showing so the other players can see them. If a player doesn't like his original roll, he can roll all five dice without penalty.

- After the second roll, each player has the poker hand he will play.

- The player with the best hand wins. If there is a tie, standard poker rules apply for the tiebreaker. Keep score with tally marks.

- Sample hands are ranked below, best to worst.
    - 5 of a kind – 2, 2, 2, 2, 2
    - 4 of a kind – 3, 3, 3, 3, 6
    - Full house – 2, 2, 2, 4, 4

- Straight – 2, 3, 4, 5, 6
- 3 of a kind – 4, 4, 4, 6, 1
- 2 of a kind – 6, 6, 5, 5, 2
- 1 pair – 1, 1, 2, 4, 6
- High card – 1, 3, 4, 5, 6

Did you know the Swedish ship *Vasa* is one of the world's most perfectly preserved shipwrecks? She sank in 1628, less than one nautical mile into her maiden voyage in the Baltic Sea. The cold water and lack of shipworms contributed to her being 95 percent intact when she was salvaged more than 300 years later in 1961.

58
Going to the Jersey Shore

The object of this game is simple: Roll a higher
total amount than the other players.

Ages: 6 and up

Number of participants: 2 or more

You'll need:
- 3 dice

How to Play:

- Select a scorekeeper, and have everyone sit in a circle in the tidal sand.

- The player who goes first has no advantage over other players. At the end of each turn, each player passes the dice to the player on his left.

- The first player rolls all three dice and sets aside the highest number rolled. He then rolls the two remaining dice and keeps the higher number. He then rolls the last die to get his total score. The scorekeeper adds up the total and writes the score in the sand.

- Play continues until each player has had a turn to roll the dice. The player with the highest total is the winner and is given a tally mark under his initials. If there's a tie, have a one-die roll-off. Highest number wins.

- The first player to win five rounds is the winner.

Did you know the best place to find sharks' teeth is not on the beach but at Shark Tooth Creek in Aliceville, Alabama? It's thought that about 70 million years ago, this 300-mile inland area was part of a barrier island. The average visitor usually finds 20 to 30 teeth during each visit.

59
Shoot the Marbles

The goal is to knock the target marbles out of the circle while keeping the shooter marble inside the circle. To successfully shoot a marble, lay the knuckles of your dominant hand on the sand, lay the marble in the crook of your index finger, and push the marble forward with your thumb.

Ages: 5 and up

Number of participants: 2 or more

You'll need:
- 1 shooter marble
- 17 smaller target marbles

How to Play:
- In the hard-packed tidal sand, lightly draw a circle 2 feet in diameter. (Expand the diameter as the players get better.)

- Place a marble in the center of the circle. Tightly pack sixteen marbles around the center marble, four marbles on four sides, in an X pattern.

- The first player rolls his shooter marble from outside the circle toward the target marbles. If a target marble is knocked out and the shooter marble stays within the circle, the player collects the target marble and gets another turn. He now shoots from where the shooter marble stopped and aims at another target marble.

- A player's turn is over when he fails to knock a target marble out or his shooter marble rolls outside the circle. If both the target and the shooter marble go outside the circle, the target marble is randomly replaced within the circle. Players continue to take turns until the last target marble has been knocked out

- The player with the most marbles is the winner.

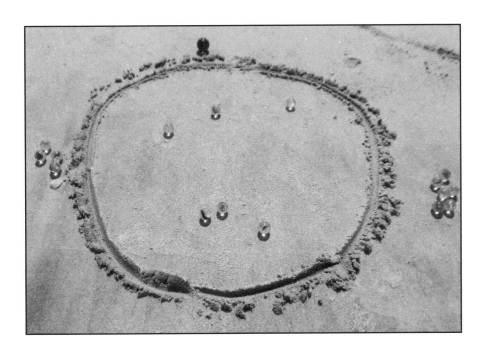

60

Marble through the Mountain

This game is like miniature golf with marbles.

Ages: 6 and up

Number of participants: 2–4

You'll need:
- 1 shooter marble
- salt hay

How to Play:
- In the tidal sand, scoop sand from an area you will not roll across to build a sand mountain 2 feet long, 6 inches high, and 4 inches wide at the base. Place salt hay around the mountain and the hole to alert beach visitors to their presence.

- With your fingers and salt hay, dig out three tunnels 1 inch wide by 1 inch high straight through the mountain. To be sure the tunnels are large enough, push the shooter marble through each hole. Smooth the sand in front of each tunnel.

- Draw a parallel shooting line 1 foot away from the mountain.

- The first player attempts to shoot the marble through the first tunnel. The marble must exit the backside of the mountain to be a successful shot. When a player makes a successful shot, he continues his turn and tries for the next tunnel. If he misses a shot, he waits for his turn again and shoots for the tunnel he advanced to.

- The first player to go through all three tunnels is the winner.
- Remember to knock the mountain down and fill in any holes when you're finished.

Did you know it might not be a bad idea to buy real estate on Iron Mountain in peninsular Florida? At an elevation of roughly 295 feet, if the sea level rose 150 feet, the area would become a tropical island.

61

Marble to the Edge

The goal of this game is to roll your marble as close to the edge of the hole without going in.

Ages: 4 and up

Number of participants: 2–6

You'll need:
- 1 marble for each player
- salt hay

How to Play:
- In the high, dry tidal sand, dig a sharp-edged semicircular gully about 6 inches long and 1 inch deep. Place salt hay on the backside of the hole to alert others to its presence.

- Draw a 2-foot-long shooting line about 4 feet away from the gully.

- Each player kneels at the shooting line and rolls his marble. If a player's marble falls into the gully, he loses the round. There is no penalty if a player knocks a previously rolled marble into the gully, causing the other marble to score no points. In fact, playing aggressively is sometimes the best strategy.

- After all players have rolled, slide your thumb along the salt hay to determine which marble is closest to the edge.

- Each round is worth 1 point. The first player who earns 10 points is the winner. The winner always goes first in the next round.

- Remember to fill in the gully when you're finished.

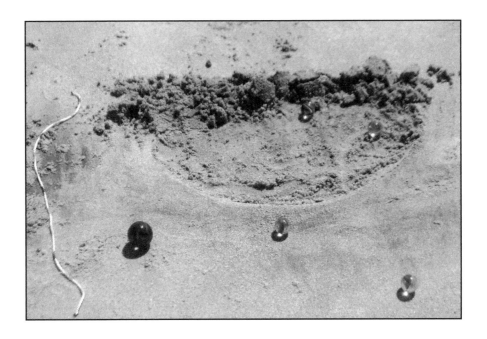

Did you know sound travels 4.3 times faster and much farther in water than in the air? In fact, submarines use the Sound Fixing and Ranging (SOFAR) channel to send messages for thousands of miles.

62

Marble Bocce

Why carry 20 pounds of bocce balls to the beach when you can carry a bag of marbles? As with bocce, the object is to shoot your marble closest to the target marble.

Ages: 7 and up
Number of participants: 2

You'll need:
- 1 shooter marble
- 3 marbles of the same color for each player

How to Play:
- Find a level spot on the hard-packed tidal sand and draw a 2-foot-long shooting line.

- Determine the shooting order. The first player shoots the target marble to a random spot 3 or 4 feet past the rolling line. He then rolls his first marble toward the target marble and is now considered "inside" or closer than the other player.

- The second player rolls his marble, trying to get closer to the target marble than the first player. He continues to roll until he is either closer than his opponent or has rolled all of his marbles. The first player then rolls again until he is inside or has rolled all of his marbles. There is no penalty for hitting the target marble or knocking other players' marbles out of the way. In fact, playing aggressively is usually the best strategy.

- After all marbles have been shot, the player whose marble is the closest to the target marble scores 1 point. If any of his other marbles are also closer to the target than his opponents', he receives an additional point for each of them.

- The first player to score 11 points is the winner.

Did you know the International Hydrographic Organization has recognized five oceans: the Arctic, Atlantic, Indian, Pacific, and Southern Oceans? The Southern Ocean was added in 2000. 〰

VIII

IF YOU BROUGHT IT . . .

When most active families pack for a trip to the coast, they throw in the bikes, golf clubs, and tennis rackets. I'm going to show you how to use those items as well as manmade beach debris in a somewhat unusual manner. Yep, we're taking it all to the beach with us.

© Jeeragone Inrut | Dreamstime.com

© Lukas Blazek | Dreamstime.com

Did you know the horseshoe crab has copper-based blood that turns blue instead of red when exposed to oxygen?

63
Golf

*Think of this as your own Sandy Beach Resort
Golf Course. We're taking golf coastal.*

Ages: 6 and up
Number of participants: 2–6

You'll need:
- putter and golf ball for each player
- salt hay

How to Play:
- In the tidal sand far away from other beach visitors, lay out a nine-hole course. Keep in mind the ball rolls faster in the high, dry tidal sand than on the damp sand near the surf.

- Use salt hay to mark each tee box, and start designing your course. For example, go 15 feet away and dig out the first hole 4 inches in diameter and 1 inch deep. Stand salt hay in the hole to serve as a flag pin and to alert other beach visitors to it.

- Let everyone's imagination run wild in designing the course. Run some holes straight down to the surf, where they may be covered by water at times. Run some holes straight uphill to the soft sand. Run some holes diagonally, and perhaps even build a dogleg around a tidal pool. (If players are young, build a relatively simple course so they don't become discouraged.)

- Near the middle of course, draw a small scorecard with each player's name and nine boxes below where you can keep score.

- As with traditional golf, players count each shot until their ball rolls into the hole. Add up the number of strokes each player takes to get his score for each hole. The player with the lowest score on the previous hole always hits first on the next hole.

- The player with fewest strokes after nine holes is the winner.

Did you know if a sea star loses one of his arms in a fight he can grow a new one?

64
Putt-Putt

Let's bring the best holes from the miniature golf course to the beach. The only thing missing is the windmill!

Ages: 6 and up
Number of participants: any

You'll need:
- putter and golf ball for each player

How to Play:
- In the hard-packed tidal sand away from other beach visitors, build the following holes.

  - Sand Volcano Hole: Build a 1-foot-square by 8-inch-high mound with a slope on one side. Place a circular 4-inch-wide by 1-inch-deep hole in the top center of the mound.
  - Whoop Section: Build six sand mounds about 10 inches apart with a gentle slope on each side. Make each one about 1 foot long by 2 inches high and 3 inches wide. Place the hole just beyond the last mound. Place the tee box 3 feet away from the first mound. Assess a two-stroke penalty for going around any of the mounds.
  - Ramp Hole: Pack sand to build a ramp 1 foot wide by 8 inches high with a gentle slope on one side. Place the hole 4 inches from the edge at the bottom

of the steep side. Place the tee box 10 feet away.

- Tidal Pool Hole: Place the tee box on one side of a small tidal pool and the hole on the other side. Assess a one-stroke penalty to remove the ball from the water; the player must replace the ball where it entered the water.
- Dogleg Hole: Place the hole behind a beach chair lying on its side, forcing the players to go around the chair to get to the hole. Place the tee box 20 feet from the hole.

- The player with the fewest strokes after all five holes is the winner.

- Remember to fill in the holes and smooth out the mounds when you're finished.

Did you know the conch fritters you ordered at the restaurant last night didn't come from Florida but from the Bahamas, Belize, or Haiti? Florida queen conchs are a federally protected species.

169

65
Roll Back

Invite the golfers in your group down to the beach to practice their putting skills.

Ages: 6 and up
Number of participants: 2

You'll need:
- salt hay
- golf ball
- 2 putters

How to Play:
- In the flatter, dry tidal sand away from other beach visitors, dig two circular 4-inch-wide by 1-inch-deep holes 10 feet apart.

- Stand salt hay behind the holes to alert beachgoers to their presence. Draw a 6-foot-long line extending 3 feet on each side of each hole to give players a tee box. This also helps protect the area in front of the holes from footprints, which could interfere with the ball's trajectory.

- Each player picks a side to hit from and attempts to hit the golf ball into the opposite hole, which counts as 1 point. After ten shots for each player, rotate sides.

- The player to sink the most putts after two rounds or twenty putts is the winner.

- Remember to fill in the holes when you're finished.

You can vary the game's difficulty by changing the distance to the holes or the size of the holes or by playing on a severely sloped section of the beach.

Did you know until 1935, North Carolina's famous Pinehurst Number 2 golf course actually had oiled sand greens? The club members said the greens were "slicker than linoleum."

66
Bicycle Coast Race

*If you have a bicycle at the beach, this is a game
the kids can play without adult supervision.*

Ages: 6 and up
Number of participants: 2 or more

You'll need:
- bicycle

How to Play:
- In the hard-packed tidal sand, mark a deep 8-foot-long line. This is where players will stop pedaling and begin coasting.

- Walk up the beach into the wind about 100 feet or 35 steps (the approximate length of a blue whale) and mark another 8-foot-long line in the sand. This will serve as the starting line. Players will have the wind at their backs as they head down the beach.

- The first player begins pedaling at the starting line and pedals as fast as he can toward the second line. When he reaches the second line, he begins coasting.

- When the bicycle will coast no farther, the rider is forced to stop. If there is only one bike, the rider writes his initials in the sand and stands there. The next player takes the bicycle to the starting line. If each player has a bicycle, the rider can stand with his bicycle until everyone has had a turn.

- The next player now takes his turn to see if he can go farther than the previous rider.
- The player who coasts the farthest is the winner.

Did you know a rogue wave almost sank the *Queen Mary* while carrying 16,000 troops in 1942? A wave estimated at 90 feet tall struck the side of the ship, causing her to list at a 52-degree angle before righting herself.

67

Tennis at the Beach

This game is a hybrid of tennis and volleyball with a few exceptions. Only one serve attempt can be made to get the ball over the net and within boundary lines. No passing between teammates is allowed, the net is in play, and a point is scored on every serve.

Ages: 8 and up

Number of participants: 2–8

You'll need:
- tennis racket for each player
- decompressed or old tennis ball
- beach volleyball court

How to Play:

You'll often find volleyball courts are empty after 5 p.m. when most beachgoers have left the beach to stand in line outside the local restaurants.

- To decompress a tennis ball, poke a pin hole in a new ball.

- Select evenly matched teams with up to four players on each team.

- The first server stands behind the back boundary line and serves the ball underhanded to the opposing team. (More experienced players may enjoy playing overhanded.) If the ball doesn't go over the net or lands outside the boundary lines, the serving team loses the right to serve and the receiving team scores a point. If the ball lands safely

within bounds, players volley until the ball is knocked out of bounds, doesn't go over the net, or hits the sand. As in volleyball, the server continues to serve until his team loses a point.

- Scoring is 15-30-40 with no advantage at 40. If both teams tie at 40, the team to score the next point wins the game.

- The first team to win six games wins the match.

> Did you know one of the oldest man-made structures on the East Coast is the 5,700-year-old Spencer's shell midden in the Florida Panhandle?

68

Sand Sock Volleyball

In this version of volleyball a player needs only to be able to catch and throw to participate. The rules and scoring are exactly like regular volleyball with three twists: There is no need to rotate players; passing to other teammates is not allowed; and all throws must be made underhanded.

Ages: 6 and up

Number of participants: 4 or more

You'll need:
- sand sock (see Beach Lingo)
- beach volleyball court

How to Play:
- Divide players into teams and have each player pick his spot to play from.
- A player standing within his team's square serves the sand sock by tossing it over the net within the boundaries to the other team.
- The receiving team must catch the sock if it's thrown within their square. The player who catches throws the sock back over the net.
- Players continue to volley until one team throws the sock out of bounds, allows the sock to land within their square, or fails to throw the sock over the net.

- As in volleyball, only the serving team can score points. Play to a predetermined total, such as 11 points, to determine the winner.

Did you know the tree known as a live oak gets its name from the fact it is an evergreen tree? This oak remains green, or "live," throughout the winter. ∽

69
Flip the Cup

The object of this game is to knock the cup onto the sand with a Frisbee. The catch? If the opposing players catch the cup before it hits the sand, it doesn't count as a point.

Ages: 10 and up
Number of participants: 4

You'll need:
- 4 wooden dowels, 4 feet long
- 4 lightweight plastic cups
- Frisbee

How to Play:
This game is best played in the soft sand, well away from other beachgoers, when there is very little wind blowing.

- Insert two dowels 1 foot into the sand side by side 24 inches apart. Twenty feet away, insert the other two dowels in the same pattern. Place a cup upside down on the top of each dowel. Test the sturdiness of the dowels by flying the Frisbee at each a few times to ensure it doesn't move.

- Each player may stand behind or beside one of the dowels. A player cannot stand in front of a dowel or interfere with the Frisbee while in flight.

- Players take turns throwing the Frisbee at their opponent's goals.

- A player can score up to 4 points on each throw. He earns 1 point if the Frisbee goes between the two upright sticks and an additional 3 points if the Frisbee knocks the cup off the stick onto the sand. If a defending player catches the cup before it hits the sand, however, the additional 3 points are not scored.

- The first team to score 10 points is the winner.

It may be necessary to occasionally reset the sticks in the sand.

Did you know the world's largest crab is the Japanese spider crab? When extended, its legs can reach up to 12 feet long. Don't worry, though—this crab is found only in the cold waters off the Japanese coastline. ☞

70
Crabbing

On the coast, you'll find crabs just about everywhere. If you're crabbing from the shoreline, be careful not to sink in the pluff mud (thick muck) or cut your feet on oyster beds.

Ages: 2 and up
Number of participants: any

You'll need:
- 20 feet of string
- chicken necks
- nylon dip net
- gloves

How to Play:
- Before you go, check the Internet for state regulations covering crabbing and determine if you need a license.

- Wrap the string around a chicken neck several times and tie it tightly with a knot.

- Toss the neck out into the water. You can hold the string in your hand or tie it to a dock railing. Let the bait sit for a few minutes and then gently pull on the string to see if there is any resistance from a crab holding on. If not, give it a few more minutes and try again. If you're still having no luck, pull the bait in and try another spot in the water.

- When you feel resistance, slowly pull the string in, trying not to spook the crab. If the line goes slack, give him a few minutes to see if he'll grab the neck again.

- When the crab gets close, use the net to bring him in and gently remove him with your gloved hands. Release the crab next to the water, but don't throw him in.

Did you know one of the world's shortest rivers is the D River in Lincoln City, Oregon? At high tide, the river flows for only 120 feet from Devil Lake into the Pacific Ocean.

IX

TRY THIS AT HOME

Even in paradise, a little rain must fall to keep the plants and flowers beautiful. If it does, that's not a problem. Here are some indoor activities to both entertain and educate the kids.

© Naumold | Dreamstime.com

Did you know one of the best surfing spots in the Southeast
is known as the Washout? This area on the northern
end of Folly Beach got its name from the fact that when
Hurricane Hugo hit South Carolina in September 1989,
it washed away most of the beachfront homes. ✍

71
Design a Dry Garden

This craft project is best completed at home, but you need to gather the materials while you're at the beach. What's the best time to hunt for seashells? Anytime you're at the beach. Well, actually, shell hunting does seem to be better within an hour of the morning's low tide.

Ages: 2 and up
Number of participants: any

You'll need:
- shells
- beach debris
- 1-gallon plastic zipper bag
- permanent marker

How to Play:
- Search the beach for the prettiest, most interesting shells and other beach debris you can find. Search in the water as well as in the storm surge wrack line in the dry sand. If there are groins on your beach, check out the spaces between the rocks. Place the items in the plastic bag as you collect them.

- After you have collected your shells, finish filling the bag with soft, dry sand. This sand will protect the shells as you transport them home and can form the base of the garden.

- Choose from a variety of containers in which to build your garden: a glass vase, a plastic box, a wicker basket, a wire bowl, a shadow box, etc. With a permanent marker on the bottom of the container, write the date and the name of the beach the shells came from. (If you have a cat at home, you probably shouldn't use an open container.)

- Pour the sand into the base and arrange the shells and other items.

Did you know the creature you found on the beach with five arms is not a starfish but a sea star? According to the National Geographic website, "Marine scientists have undertaken the difficult task of replacing the beloved starfish's common name with sea star because, well, the starfish is not a fish. It's an echinoderm, closely related to sea urchins and sand dollars." ≈

72

Ocean in a Bottle

This project takes only a moment to complete but will provide hours of fun for younger children.

Ages: 2 and up

Number of participants: any

You'll need:
- funnel
- sand
- small shells
- empty clear plastic bottle with a cap
- water
- blue food coloring
- cooking oil

How to Play:
- Using a funnel, pour the sand and small shells into the bottle until it's one-fifth full.

- Add tap water until it's three-fifths full, and then add four drops of food coloring.

- Fill the bottle the rest of the way with cooking oil, and screw the cap on tightly.

- Lay the bottle on its side and let the different ingredients settle into their respective layers.

Did you know sea foam forms naturally as pounding waves churn up seafloor sediments such as dissolved salts, proteins, and other organic matter? ✐

73
Float an Egg

The goal is to observe the difference between fresh and salt water.

Ages: 5 and up
Number of participants: any

You'll need:
- measuring cup
- 2 plastic cups
- 3 tablespoons of salt
- 1 fresh egg in the shell
- freezer

How to Play:
- Pour 8 ounces of tap water into each plastic cup. Stir salt into one of the cups. Gently place the egg in the cup of tap water. Remove the egg and then place it in the saltwater mixture. Remove the egg. The egg should have sunk to the bottom of the tap water and should have floated in the salt water because of the different densities of the two waters. The egg is denser than the tap water, but the salt water has a greater density than the egg, allowing the egg to float.

- Place both cups in the freezer overnight.

- In the morning, the tap water should be frozen solid, but the salt water should be no more than slushy. This is because salt molecules are excluded from the freezing process, so as the water molecules freeze, the salt content in the remaining water becomes even saltier. Instead of freezing at 32°, this even saltier water now requires a much lower temperature to freeze.

Three tablespoons of salt in 8 ounces of water is a super concentration. Ordinary seawater, at 35 grams of salt per 1,000 grams of water, will freeze around 28.6°F.

Did you know the Sullivan's Island Lighthouse near Charleston was the last major lighthouse to be built by the federal government? When activated on June 15, 1962, the lighthouse featured an amazing 28-million-candlepower light, which was the second brightest light in the Western Hemisphere. The original light, which was later downgraded, created so much heat that the lightkeepers had to wear welding suits when they entered the lantern room. ∞

74
Let's See Density in Action

Now that we've seen an egg float, let's get a visual understanding of why it happened.

Ages: 2 and up

Number of participants: any

You'll need:
- two small drinking glasses
- water
- measuring cup
- tablespoon
- salt
- eyedropper
- red food coloring
- cooler (optional)
- unopened can of diet soda
- unopened can of non-diet soda

How to Play:
- Fill one glass halfway with tap water. Using the measuring cup, pour 4 ounces of tap water into the other glass.
- Place 2 tablespoons of salt in the glass with 4 ounces of water and stir the mixture. Add four drops of red food coloring to the saltwater mixture and stir again.
- Fill the eyedropper with the saltwater mixture and place four drops in the glass of tap water. The red salt water

190

should sink to the bottom of the glass. Since density is measured by how closely molecules are packed together, the salt water sinks because the salt particles fill in the gaps between the water molecules.

- For a real-world example of density at work, fill a cooler or sink with 8 inches of tap water. Place the unopened soft drink cans in the water. Ask kids to guess which one will float.

Even though the cans are identical in volume, the diet drink floats while the regular drink sinks. The reason? The regular drink has up to 40 grams of added sugar. Just like the salt particles, these dissolved sugar particles add to the density but not to the volume.

Did you know in 1883 almost nine miles of Charleston, South Carolina, streets were paved with cobblestones? The stones were used as ballast weights to keep merchant ships stable as they sailed the ocean from Europe and the Northeast.

75

Ocean Currents

In Let's See Density in Action, we saw that denser salt water sank in fresh water. Now let's look at how cold water affects the ocean's currents.

Ages: 2 and up
Number of participants: any

You'll need:
- baking pan
- water
- sandwich bag
- sand
- ice cubes
- red food coloring

How to Play:
- Fill a baking pan halfway with warm tap water and place it in a level spot.
- Fill the bottom of a sandwich bag with sand and finish filling the bag with ice cubes. Seal the bag and place it in the pan.
- Place two drops of food coloring in front of the ice bag and wait for the results.

The food coloring should begin to leave a trail that moves in a straight line away from the ice. This is the beginning of a current, which is the same thing that happens on a global scale as cold water moves away from the ice on polar ice caps. The same thing happens along the equator as water warmed by the sun begins to move, forming currents such as the Gulf Stream.

Did you know one of the foggiest places in the world is the Grand Banks off the coast of Newfoundland? The cold water of the Labrador Current meets the warm water from the Gulf Stream. The Grand Banks was one of the world's most productive fishing areas before industrialized fishing decimated the fish population.

76
Make Your Own Sea Salt

We're going to use the sun to help us understand why ocean water tastes salty. Because of the windy conditions at the beach, this is best done at home or in your hotel room.

Ages: 2 and up

Number of participants: any

You'll need:
- empty water bottle
- measuring cup
- saucer
- food coloring (optional)
- salt water

How to Play:
- Wade into the ocean about chest deep where the sand isn't being churned up by the waves, and fill the water bottle. Pass the bottle around to let everyone see how clear seawater actually is.

- Pour 1 ounce of seawater into the saucer and add a dash of food coloring if you like.

- Place the saucer in a sunny spot where rain and dust won't contaminate the water.

After a while, you should find the water gone and salt crystals in the bottom of the saucer. If you added food coloring, the salt crystals will be easier to see. The kids may ask, "How did the salt get there when the water was so clear?" Water is one of nature's greatest solvents. The water breaks down the bonds of the salt's sodium and chloride molecules, allowing them to be invisible to the naked eye. But since these elements don't evaporate as easily as the water molecules, when the water evaporates, the sodium and chloride molecules are free to rejoin into salt crystals. This is a simplified version our ancestors have used to manufacture sea salt for thousands of years. (Remember that this salt is an unrefined product, so don't use it on your steak tonight.)

Did you know the human body contains salt? Have you ever tasted your own sweat?

77

The Water Cycle

This experiment will give kids an understanding
of how Earth's water cycle works.

Ages: 2 and up

Number of participants: any

You'll need:
- tall drinking glass
- measuring cup
- water
- microwave oven
- sandwich bag
- rubber band
- 3 ice cubes

How to Play:
- To represent warm ocean water, pour 4 ounces of tap water into a clear glass. Microwave the water on high for 30 seconds.

- Remove the glass immediately. Place the sandwich bag inside the glass, forming a cup, and fold the outer edges of the bag over the rim of the glass. To seal in the water vapor, wrap the rubber band around the bag on the outside of the glass. Place the ice cubes inside the bag.

- Place the glass on a counter and come back in 1 hour.

You should notice that condensation has formed on both the bottom of the bag and the sides of the glass. This condensation is water vapor that has drifted up from the warm water into the cold upper atmosphere, represented by the ice cubes. The condensation will collect in the clouds and return to Earth as rain.

Did you know many coastal cities, such as Tampa, Florida, use desalination plants to supply their fresh water? The Tampa Bay Seawater Desalination Plant uses reverse osmosis to produce up to 25 million gallons of fresh water daily.

RECOMMENDED READING

Ballantine, Todd. *Tideland Treasure.* Columbia, SC: University of South Carolina Press, 1991.

Bostick, Douglas W., and Jason R. Davidson. *The Boathouse: Tales and Recipes from a Southern Kitchen.* Charleston, SC: Joggling Board Press, 2006.

Casey, Susan. *The Wave: In Pursuit of the Rogues, Freaks, and Giants of the Ocean.* New York: Anchor Books, 2010.

Cerullo, Mary M. *Sea Turtles: Ocean Nomads.* New York: Dutton Children's Books, 2003.

Coenraads, Robert R. *Rocks and Fossils: A Visual Guide.* Buffalo, NY: Firefly Books, Ltd., 2005.

Collier, Michael. *Over the Coasts: An Aerial View of Geology.* New York: Mikaya Press, Inc., 2009.

Drake, Jane. *Kids Summer Games Book.* Buffalo, NY: Kids Can Press, 1998.

Earle, Sylvia A. *The World Is Blue: How Our Fate and the Ocean's Are One.* Washington, DC: National Geographic Society, 2009.

Fox, William T. *At the Sea's Edge: An Introduction to Coastal Oceanography for the Amateur Naturalist.* Upper Saddle River, NJ: Prentice-Hall, 1983.

Ganeri, Anita. *I Wonder Why the Sea Is Salty and Other Questions about the Oceans.* New York: Kingfisher, 2011.

Gordon, Lynn. *52 Fun Things to Do at the Beach.* San Francisco: Chronicle Books, 1999.

Grunfeld, Frederic V. *Games of the World: How to Make Them, How to Play Them, How They Came to Be.* Versailles, KY: Rand McNally Company, 1975.

Hill, Leonard. *Shells: Treasures of the Sea.* Fairfield, CT: Hugh Lauter Levin Associates Inc., 1996.

Hubal, Jim, and Joanne Hubal. *A Week at the Beach: 100 Life-changing Things You Can Do by the Seashore.* New York: Marlowe & Company, 2003.

Hutchinson, Stephen, and Lawrence E. Hawkins. *Oceans: A Visual Guide.* Buffalo, NY: Firefly Books Ltd., 2008.

Kusky, Timothy, Ph.D. *The Coast: Hazardous Interactions within the Coastal Environment.* New York: Facts on File, 2008.

———. *Tsunamis: Giant Waves from the Sea.* New York: Facts on File, 2008.

Leifermann, Henry. *Compass American Guides: South Carolina.* 4th ed. New York: Fodor's Travel Publications, 2006.

Louv, Richard. *Last Child in the Woods: Saving Our Children from Nature-deficit Disorder.* Chapel Hill, NC: Algonquin Books of Chapel Hill, 2005.

Love, Ann, and Jane Drake. Kids and Grandparents: An Activity Book. Niagara Falls, NY: Kids Can Press, 2000.

Meyer, Peter. Nature Guide to the Carolina Coast: Common Birds, Crabs, Shells, Fish, and other Entities of the Coastal Environment. Wilmington, NC: Avian-Cetacean Press, 1991.

Mullarkey, Lisa. *Splashing by the Shore: Beach Activities for Kids.* Layton, UT: Gibbs Smith, 2007.

Parker, Bruce. *The Power of the Sea,: Tsunamis, Storm Surges, Rogue Waves, and Our Quest to Predict Disasters.* New York: Palgrave Macmillan, 2010.

Parker, Steve. *100 Things You Should Know about the Seashore.* Broomall, PA: Mason Crest Publishers, 2011.

Pellant, Chris. *Rocks, Minerals & Fossils of the World.* New York: Little, Brown & Company, 1990.

Pollack, Henry, Ph.D. *A World without Ice.* New York: The Penguin Group, 2009.

Prager, Ellen J., with Sylvia A. Earle. *The Oceans.* New York: McGraw-

Hill, 2000.

Rhyne, Nancy. *Carolina Seashells*. Orangeburg, SC: Sandlapper Publishing, Inc., 1997.

Riley, Peter D. *Survivor's Science on an Island*.Chicago: Heinemann-Raintree, 2005.

Ripoll, Oriol. Play with Us: 100 Games from around the World. Chicago: Chicago Review Press, 2005.

Staub, Frank. *Sea Turtles*. Minneapolis, MN. Lerner Publications Co., 1995.

Stott, Dorothy. *The Big Book of Games*. New York: Dutton Children's Books, 1998.

Strother, Scott. *The Adventurous Book of Outdoor Games: Classic Fun for Daring Boys and Girls*. Naperville, IL. Sourcebooks, Inc., 2008.

Van Rose, Susanna. *DK Eyewitness Books: Earth*. New York: DK Publishing, Inc., 2005.

Whitty, Julia. *Deep Blue Home: An Intimate Ecology of Our Wild Ocean*. New York: Houghton Mifflin Harcourt, 2010.

Wierenga, Lucinda. *Sandcastles Made Simple: Step-by-Step Instructions, Tips, and Tricks for Building Sensational Sand Creations*. New York: Stewart, Tabori & Chang, 2009.

Winchester, Simon. *Atlantic: Great Sea Battles, Heroic Discoveries, Titanic Storms, and a Vast Ocean of a Million Stories*. New York: HarperCollins Publishers, 2010.

Wise, Debra. *Great Big Book of Children's Games: Over 450 Indoor and Outdoor Games for Kids*. Pleasantville, NY: Round Stone Press, 1999.

Witherington, Blair, and Dawn Witherington. *Seashells of Georgia and the Carolinas: A Beachcomber's Guide*. Sarasota, FL: Pineapple Press, 2011.

Here are some other books from Pineapple Press on related topics. For a complete catalog, write to Pineapple Press, P.O. Box 3889, Sarasota, Florida 34230-3889, or call (800) 746-3275. Or visit our website at www.pineapplepress.com.

Florida's Living Beaches by Blair and Dawn Witherington. Comprehensive accounts of more than 800 species found along 700 miles of Florida's sandy beaches. Includes plants, animals, minerals, and manmade objects, each accompanied by a color photo.

Living Beaches of Georgia and the Carolinas by Blair and Dawn Witherington. Comprehensive listing of more than 850 items along 600 miles of Atlantic coastline. More than 1,000 color photos highlight birds, turtles, fish, mammals, flowers, and much more. Meticulously researched, this is an attractive and handy guidebook for beachgoers.

Florida's Seashells by Blair and Dawn Witherington. Identifies more than 250 species of mollusks, each accompanied by a color photo, range map, and description. This slim volume will fit perfectly in your beach bag.

Seashells of Georgia and the Carolinas by Blair and Dawn Witherington. Full-color photos throughout illustrate hundreds of the shells you'll find on the beaches of Georgia and the Carolinas. Includes details about the features, habitat, and diet of each shell's inhabitant.

Florida's Birds, Second Edition, by David Maehr and Herbert Kale II. Beautifully illustrated by Karl Karalus, this full-color guide contains sections on bird study, feeding, habitats, threatened and endangered species, exotics, and conservation.

Common Coastal Birds of Florida and the Caribbean by David Nellis. Features 72 birds that inhabit the zone where the sea meets the land. Includes feeding habits, reproduction, behavior, migration, predators, longevity, and conservation issues as well as a full-color section.

Seasons of the Sea by Jay Humphreys. As the seasons change on land, so do they in the waters along the Florida peninsula, a world largely unknown but endlessly fascinating. Learn what creatures come and go in the waters of each of the state's six main regions. Charming illustrations accompany the text.

Coastal North Carolina, Second Edition, by Terrance Zepke. Find quick histories of islands, towns, and regions; main attractions; opportunities for recreation, sports, and outdoor activities; and festivals and events. Includes trivia, quizzes, and even a few ghost stories.

Coastal South Carolina by Terrance Zepke. From Myrtle Beach to Beaufort, South Carolina's Lowcountry is steeped in history and full of charm. Includes brief histories and fast facts for the islands and communities, historical and current photos of local attractions, calendars of events, helpful maps, and tourism resources.

Seashore Plants of South Florida and the Caribbean by David Nellis. A complete source for both serious naturalists and backyard gardeners who want to learn which plants grow best in nearshore environments. Includes for each plant: form, flower, and fruit date; geographical distribution; habitat; reproduction; propagation; and medicinal, edible, and toxic aspects.

Dangerous Sea Life of the West Atlantic, Caribbean, and Gulf of Mexico by Edwin Iversen and Renate Skinner. Learn how to avoid dangerous creatures and administer first aid. Sections on species that bite and sting, pests that harm swimmers, toxic species, and fish-beak injuries.

Poisonous Plants and Animals of Florida and the Caribbean by David Nellis. A nontechnical guide that provides in-depth information on the toxins, symptoms, and treatments for each plant and animal, as well as beneficial uses and folklore.

Florida Magnificent Wilderness by James Valentine and D. Bruce Means. World-famous nature photographer Valentine presents art images of the state's remote wilderness areas. Comprehensive text by biologist Means and other Florida conservationists rounds out this beautiful volume.

NOTES

NOTES

NOTES

NOTES

NOTES